A NEW YORKER'S NEW YORK

A NEW YORKER'S NEW YORK

KARIM GEIST

CHÊNE

SUMMARY

> *"One belongs to New York instantly, one belongs to it as much in five minutes as in five years."*
>
> **Tom Wolfe**

I lived in New York City for 25 years, and a large part of me belongs to it. This majestic, amazing, almost surreal city captivates the dreams of people from all over the world who want to discover and fall in love with it. In my youth, I decided to make it my mistress. I grew up with her, matured with her, and have never stopped loving her. I've known her intimately: I saw her early in the morning, when she wasn't yet clean, still hungover from the night before; and during the day, frantic, in an eternal sprint to please the world; we met up again at night, beautiful, sparkling, encouraging the craziness that she alone could offer. My city, my first love, I shared her with the masses, but I felt like she was mine.

I'd like my friends from elsewhere to discover the places that make the city the enchanting sorceress she is, the places that have brought me so much pleasure and provided so many lasting memories. Wherever you are in the world, when you come to New York, I want you to be able to live the city as I have, taking advantage of each secret to enjoy it to the very last drop. This book is also an invitation to my city friends to rediscover their own backyard: hit the pause button on the constant pursuit of the latest opening and the next best thing to remember the extraordinary luck you have to live in the most incredible city in the world.

Let's take the time to cherish the places that make up the true soul of this city. We have to support them to ensure that the authentic heart of the city continues to beat a while longer against the onslaught of passing fads.

This book is your instruction manual on how to belong to New York, the advice of one New Yorker to another. Run with it.

Karim Geist

Downtown Manhattan

South Street Seaport.

Financial District

BREAKFAST

Breakfast is the most overlooked meal for New Yorkers. The "power breakfast," the morning meeting of businessmen seen more often in old films than in real life, may still exist, but more often than not, breakfast is reduced to no more than splashes of coffee spilling out of a torn plastic cover. Today, several restaurants have come around to realizing that there is a clientele demanding more than a bagel swallowed on the run between the subway and the office.

Balthazar

80 Spring Street, New York, NY 10012
(212) 965-1414

For many New Yorkers, Keith McNally's crown jewel is the epitome of the French brasserie, with its authentic French cuisine. Due to its unrelenting popularity, snagging a comfortable booth for lunch or dinner can get tricky, however, at breakfast, which starts at 7:30am, the place has a subdued air about it. Selecting from one of the many egg selections is always a good choice as it frees you up to overindulge in the out of this world breadbasket, especially the *brioche*. The cost of this breakfast runs a bit high but you can't really put a price on this pleasure.

Buvette

42 Grove Street, New York, NY 10014
(212) 255-3590

Buvette is another place that, while tightly packed at night with neighborhood regulars sipping wine and nibbling on small plates, is pleasantly sedate in the mornings. They serve a breakfast excellently split into four sections: pastries, tartines, waffles and crepes, with three odd egg dishes to boot. The piece de resistance is the espresso-machine-steamed eggs, which are exactly what they sound like. It's not just the plates that are charming though: a marble bar, reclaimed white oak flooring and a chandelier custom made by artist Warren Muller are all more noticeable during breakfast hours, which run from 8am well into the afternoon.

Clinton Street Baking Company

4 Clinton St, New York, NY 10002
(646) 602-6263

Clinton St. Baking Company is renowned for its pancakes, and for good reason. You can expect long lines of people eager to enjoy their fluffy, perfect flapjacks and moist, flavorful scones. The buttermilk-biscuit sandwich with scrambled eggs and

PARIS
28 rue henry monnier
SOUTH PIGALLE
NEW YORK
42 grove street
WEST VILLAGE
i love buvette.com

bacon is also a revelation. Clinton St. Baking Company started as a breakfast and brunch spot and then had to expand to lunch and dinner in order to satisfy demand, the result being that you can now get your pancake fix day and night. On weekends, it's not unusual to wait more than an hour for a seat in the tiny restaurant, so take advantage of a weekday morning.

Joseph Leonard

170 Waverly Pl, New York, NY 10014
(646) 429-8383

Joseph Leonard is a West Village hot spot at night and especially on weekends, when people line up for the chance to brunch. The cozy space feels like a long-lost restaurant from another era, with a wooden ceiling, rough-hewn wooden floorboards and walls bedecked with everything from a vintage exit sign to vintage trunks, photographs, art and antique mirrors. Joseph Leonard is known for its excellent Ethiopian coffee and inventive egg dishes, but also for its ability to turn brussels sprouts into appealing early morning fare.

Shopsin's

120 Essex St, New York, NY 10002

If you're looking for an "only in NYC" breakfast experience, look no further than the legendary Shopsin's, located on the South side of the Essex Market.

No reservations, no groups larger than 4, and no ordering the same thing as someone else at your table. At one point, Shopsin's had a menu boasting nearly 1000 items, and though it's been trimmed a bit, a fact you couldn't be expected to guess after looking at the still insane menu, all of the craziest breakfast combinations you could imagine are still there, like the *Mo'Betta*, which has maple bacon and scrambled eggs sandwiched together by Shopsin's famous mac n' cheese pancakes. You don't come to Shopsin's for a tranquil and healthy start to your day. Shopsin's isn't open Monday and Tuesday.

Egg

109 N 3ʳᵈ St, Brooklyn, NY 11249
(718) 302-5151

Unlike in many other countries, eggs are the foundation of the traditional American breakfast, so it would make sense to head to a place whose very name pays tribute to the breakfast jewel. Although this requires a descent into the Valley of Hipster, the journey is well worth it, as proven by the hour-long waits on weekends. But again, the hustle and bustle is non-existent weekdays, when they open at 7am. Order up some coffee, which comes to you in an individually brewed French press for extra quaintness points, and try the phenomenal *Eggs Rothko* (a thick slice of brioche with an egg cooked in the middle, all covered in a blanket of melted Grafton cheddar).

COCKTAILS BARS

For years, exclusive speakeasy style cocktail dens were reserved for the elite, the masses preferring to settle for a cold brew at the local pub instead of duking it out for a reservation in a clandestine bar. The city's cocktail craze has exploded though and the culture has been rebranded, so on a night when you can't deny the call of a well-balanced cocktail served in a fancy glass, there are now plenty of destinations that no longer require knowing which doorbell to ring or password to whisper. Some of the best bartenders in the world ply their trade in New York, offering tastes of spirits and crafting bespoke cocktails.

Mayahuel

304 E 6th St, New York, NY 10003
(212) 253-5888

Tequila, and its cousin, mescal, are the stars at Mayahuel, a bijoux treasure of a bar in the East Village. Try one of the strange stirrings, like *The Lux-Capacitor* (reposado tequila, Nonino & Luxardo amaros, Oloroso sherry & grapefruit essence), or explore Mexican terroir through a tasting flight. Don't forget a bite or two while you're at it; the *cochinita* — braised pork belly with papaya mango mustard — is not to be missed and neither are the churros.

Pouring Ribbons

225 Avenue B, New York, NY 10009
(917) 656-6788

Located above a liquor store, the cocktail den offers a refreshing dose of unpretentiousness. Here, Joaquín Simó,

Tales of the Cocktail 2012 American Bartender of the Year, has pledged to put guests on a "pedestal of equal importance as the cocktails." The cocktail menu is broken down in two scales: refreshing to spirituous and comforting to adventurous, a standout being the *Gung Hey Fat Choy*. Whatever you order, rest assured that if the scale tips too far towards the spirituous, you can always seek to balance things out with one of the delicious plates crafted by Beecher's Handmande Cheese.

Weather Up

589 Vanderbilt Avenue, Brooklyn, NY 11238
weatherupnyc.com

The cocktail list is minimalistic but perfectly thought out, featuring a selection of ten expertly mixed choices which combine classics and more experimental creations. In the warmer months, be sure not to miss the back garden.

Dead Rabbit Grocery & Grog

30 Water St, New York, NY 10004
(646) 422-7906

At Dead Rabbit, the menu focuses on interpretations of drinks dating from the 1600s to the late 1800s, including punches. Each drink here has been historically researched, then tweaked for the modern palate, and while it can be a little daunting to peruse a menu full of ingredients you've never heard of, the complimentary punch served to all customers, an amuse-bouche of sorts, gets you in the mood and also makes waiting for your order more pleasant. The trek is worth it to experience the 2013 winner for World's Best Cocktail Menu.

Death & Company

433 E 6th St, New York, NY 10009
(212) 388-0882

Death & Company manages to be sophisticated without being stuffy: the dimly lit intimate interior exudes a cool, jazzy vibe. With an extensive menu, you're in for a treat whether you're a cocktail newbie or a seasoned imbiber. Your cocktail will be stirred up to 50 times, and it's a good sign to see it meticulously taste tested by the bartenders. Here, even martinis stand out, as they are served in six-ounce glasses with the remainder poured into iced carafes so they stay chilled until you're ready. When you need a little sustenance ordering up a portion of the truffled mac & cheese or the molten chocolate cake is a no brainer.

Cienfuegos

95 Avenue A, New York, NY 10009
(212) 614-6818

Cienfuegos, a place whose look can best be described as cross between *Alice in Wonderland* and 1950's Cuba, is known for being the first bar in New York to develop an entirely punch based drink menu. These drinks can be ordered as single cocktails, in a larger "Amigos" size, a still larger "Familia", and all the way up to the "Royale", which is big enough for a group of ten to share. The cocktails are divided into categories like fizzes, "big and bold," "the spice of life," and "Papa's list" - a reference to Ernest Hemingway, a section that of course includes the classic daiquiri.

THE PERFECT MANHATTAN

The Manhattan evokes the golden age of cocktail history. Back when New York City meant Manhattan, the eponymous cocktail was the king of all cocktails and was prepared with rye whiskey made in the state of New York itself, which until Prohibition was home to more than 1,200 distilleries.

Now this cocktail can be found expertly prepared all over the world, but to enjoy it in its natural environment, I like to go to Bemelmans Bar at the Carlyle Hotel on the Upper East Side.

Sitting at the bar among the murals painted by Ludwig Bemelman, creator of the Madeleine series of children's books, you can build a bridge between the past and the present by specifying that you want your Manhattan "perfect," a variation on the classic using equal parts "sweet" and "dry" vermouth.

To take a little piece of the city's history home with you, just follow these instructions:

The Perfect Manhattan

(Makes one cocktail)

2oz Tuthilltown Hudson Manhattan rye whiskey
.5oz Carpano Antica sweet vermouth
.5oz Dolin dry vermouth
3 drops of orange bitters
Lemon zest

Pour the ingredients into a mixing glass, add five large cubes of ice and stir vigorously with a mixing spoon.
Strain into a pre-chilled glass and garnish with a lemon zest.

BRUNCH

For New Yorkers, brunch has become something resembling a civic duty, and it's without a doubt one of our favorite weekend pastimes. Brunch is also no longer considered just a Sunday thing: you've got your festive Saturday brunches with bottomless booze, your classic Sunday brunch, and even Monday industry brunches for those who worked all weekend making sure the rest of us had fun. It's not unusual to brunch twice either: Saturday to start the weekend and Sunday to relax, and whether you're looking for a $10 or $1,000 brunch, the city's got you covered.

PARTY BRUNCH

Beaumarchais

409 West 13th Street, New York, NY 10014
(212) 675-2400

Beaumarchais is famous for its Grand Brunch, an unbridled afternoon celebration when the volume goes up, the lights go down, and the bistro breaks into an explosion of table dancing.

At this unique brasserie, banquette tables are made for dancing and the Champagne magnums are made for both drinking and dousing. The brunch boasts delicacies such as homemade *foie gras* plumped with a Calvados and apple cider filling and a savory *Croque Madame* lavished with truffled *béchamel*, and with a list of over 20 Champagnes by the bottle to order from, you'll be feeling like royalty in no time.

Beaumarchais

LAVO

39 East 58ᵗʰ Street, New York, NY 10022
(212) 750-5588

Originally inspired by brunch parties held along the Cote d'Azur, Lavo's brunch attracts an international crowd comprised primarily of the one percent. It all starts out pretty calmly: people arrive around 2:00 p.m. and settle down to enjoy as much of their meal as possible before the lights start to dim around 3:30pm.
The lights dim gradually and the volume of the music rises over the course of an hour as the energy level of the songs slowly increases. Before you know it- you're dancing on a table and getting sprayed with a bottle of Dom Perignon.

SUNDAY BRUNCH

ABC Cocina

38 East 19ᵗʰ Street, New York, NY 10003
(212) 677-2233

Michelin starred Chef Jean-Georges Vongerichten's Nuevo Latino establishment. The restaurant itself is stunning: depression-era vintage glass, reclaimed wood, steel tables, energy-efficient LED lighting and hot pink mismatched chairs. ABC Cocina's brunch menu has several sandwiches, plus breakfast dishes like *huevos rancheros*, Mexican-spiced French toast, and coconut pancakes. But the best thing to do at ABC Cocina is to order enough vegetable plates, seafood starters, and fried snacks for everyone to share.

Sarabeth's

Multiple locations throughout the city
www.sarabeths.com

For the breakfast we all wish we were lucky enough to have every weekend as kids, Sarabeth's is the savior. The classic brunch fare includes fluffy omelets folded around fresh fillings vibrant with flavor along with scrambled and Benedict choices, waffles and pancakes, and oatmeals and granolas. A standout is the nod to the Jewish brunch tradition of bagels and lox, the "Goldie Lox" omelet, not to be overlooked.
Most of the egg dishes come with a choice of muffin or scone as well as Sarabeth's famous preserves.

BRUNCH IN BROOKLYN

Henry Public

329 Henry Street, Brooklyn, NY 11201
(718) 852-8630

With a killer menu featuring their delicious "Hamburger Sandwiches" and the famous *Turkey Leg Sandwich*, shelling out a couple extra bucks for a Bloody Henry, their version of the classic brunch cocktail they make with shallot infused vodka and celery bitters, should justify a visit to Cobble Hill. The saloon itself is classic in appearance, with tables for two and low lighting, and whether you choose to sit at the bar up front or the dining room in the back, a friendly staff will make you feel like you're family and the hearty menu will ensure you come back again and again.

ALL YOU CAN DRINK BRUNCHES

Paradou

8 Little West 12th St, Manhattan, NY 10014
(212) 463-8345

You'll enter the ivy-covered blue doors of this peaceful Meatpacking District retreat to discover a rustic, friendly atmosphere. A fun place for larger groups, Paradou offers The Unlimited Champagne Cocktail Brunch, an undeniably attractive option. The menu doesn't disappoint either, with standouts that include the *Wake & Bake* (creamy polenta, two sunny-side eggs, and andouille sausage, topped with gruyere cheese) and the *Really Big Lamb Burger* (seasoned ground lamb topped with goat cheese and figs, served with sautéed fingerling potatoes).

Poco

33 Avenue B, New York, NY 10009
(212) 228-4461

Sitting pretty in Alphabet City is Poco, a Spanish inspired restaurant with an affordable brunch special. For $30, you have your choice of entrée accompanied by an unlimited supply of mimosas, Bloody Marys and sangria and three hours to enjoy them. The brunch menu features a variety of classic Spanish choices, like the *Poco Benedict* (crispy arepa, chorizo, manchego cheese and poached eggs, topped with pimentón hollandaise), as well as American standbys, including the to die for *Lobster Mac n Cheese* (manchego, asiago and Parmesan, topped with crunch panko). The music is catchy and loud, but not so overbearing.

MOVIE THEATERS

One of my favorite things to do in life has always been to go to the movies, to sit in a dark theater, eating popcorn and being transported through the big screen into another world. On a rainy day, while the latest romantic comedy draws in the crowds at the multiplex, heading to one of the city's art houses or old school theaters can be the perfect way to inject some culture without battling the flocks of tourists at the museums.

Angelika Film Center & Café

18 West Houston Street, New York, NY 10012
(212) 995-2570

The Angelika Film Center is probably New York City's best-known cinema for fans of independent films and since 1989 is in large part responsible for helping to make "indies" the vibrant part of the film industry. On the six screens located downstairs you'll find provocative film festival selections from Sundance to Venice while on the entire first floor, the café is perhaps the most critical part of what has made the Angelika a success. No ordinary popcorn stand, the café features cappuccino, panini, gourmet cakes, and vegan cookies from Sacred Chow.

Paris Theater

4 West 58th Street, New York, NY 10019
(212) 688-3800

The Paris Theatre opened on September 13, 1948, with Marlene Dietrich cutting the ribbon in the presence of the Ambassador to France, and as its name implies, the Paris has an affinity for playing foreign films, especially French films. It is the longest continually operating art cinema in the United States, one of the last single-screen art houses around, and one of those classic Manhattan gems that you visit once in a blue moon and wonder why you don't go there more often. The Paris belongs to a different era, one when people would dress up to go to the movies, and makes for one of the best date night destinations in New York.

Film Forum

209 West Houston Street, New York, NY 10014
(212) 727-8110

The Film Forum is New York City's only autonomous nonprofit movie theater, and though it has famously cramped seating, it makes up for it by showing films of yesteryear, many themed together, like Spaghetti Westerns, French New Wave flicks or films scored by Ennio Morricone. Fresh kernels are popped in peanut oil and nothing else: the only topping on offer here is sea salt and really, it's all you'll need.

Film Society

165 West 65th Street, New York, 10023
(212) 875-5610

The Film Society is located at the Walter Reade Theatre at Lincoln Center and offers a solid mix of specialty and regular programming, showing independent and foreign films in addition to more mainstream showcases. Worth checking out is the $25 Dinner-and-a-Movie deal, which pairs an independent film with food and wine from Lincoln Center's restaurant. The theaters themselves are definitely some of the nicest in New York, with funky paneling, super-clean seats and sleek LCD screens.

Landmark Sunshine Theater

143 East Houston Street, New York, NY 10002
(212) 260-7289

The Sunshine is a historic building reborn as a comfortable art house theater (stadium seating is a welcome change from some other independents). Formerly a Yiddish vaudeville house, this theater now houses intimate cinemas with excellent sound that makes for a beautiful complement to the well-curated mix of new independent films and goofy midnight classics it screens, with highlights including midnight showings of *Space Jam, Pulp Fiction* or the *Evil Dead series*. Another thing setting this theater apart is that the popcorn is popped in a blend of coconut and corn oils and butter-flavored salt, giving it

a slightly more robust flavor and you can choose from ten different toppings, including parmesan and garlic, Cajun or chocolate marshmallow.

Nighthawk Cinema

136 Metropolitan Avenue, Brooklyn, NY 11249
(718) 384-3980

Michelin-starred chef Saul Bolton of Boerum Hill restaurant Saul has put his culinary vision into designing the menu at the café attached Nitehawk Cinema. Arrive 30 minutes before your flick starts to grab menus and a table for two. Your waiter will take your order, but once the light goes down, you'll have to make food requests quietly, via pen and paper. About 45 minutes before the movie ends, the unobtrusive staff will bring your check, which also serves as last call. Alongside choices such as homemade jerky made with lime, Thai chili and ginger, fish tacos, and other small plates, the menu includes specials made for each specific film: *The Godfather* was paired with an orange themed menu while *The Rum Diary* menu included a rum raisin bread pudding. And now that a law forbidding the serving of alcohol in movie theaters has been repealed, cocktails based on the movies are available, as well as a selection of craft beers, to be enjoyed before, during and after the movie.

STEAK HOUSES

There are times in a man's life when he needs to get back in touch with his roots, connect with the true carnivore inside, and those times call for a great steak. New York City is full of steak houses that will satisfy that desire. We have grand expectations of our steak houses, so when the time comes to slice a steak knife into a juicy slab of meat, these are the standard bearers.

Benjamin Steak House

52 East 41st Street, New York, NY 10017
(212) 297-9177

Benjamin Steak House is the kind of place you can imagine the Mad Men frequenting and then hunkering down in front of a thick slab of meat before boarding their trains back to the suburbs. The brainchild of Arturo McLeod, who perfected his grilling technique at Peter Luger, Benjamin Steak House has the elegant surroundings to contrast the straightforward punch of the steak on the plate. High ceilings, brass chandeliers, oak paneling and leather seating provide the perfect setting in which to enjoy these hefty cuts of beef.

Keens

72 West 36th Street, Manhattan, NY 10018
(212) 947-3636

Keens is a portal to a bygone era as much as it is a restaurant. The ceilings of the various dining rooms, are decorated with hanging pipes, even including those that belonged to famous patrons such as Babe Ruth and Theodore Roosevelt. Vintage photographs, political cartoons and theater bills cover the walls around you. In addition to the gargantuan slabs of meat, the bar at Keens also stocks upwards of 100 different Scotches, the perfect way to add a little smokiness to your plate.

Sparks Steak House

210 East 46th Street, New York, NY 10017
(212) 687-4855

Sparks gained international notoriety in 1985 when Paul Castellano of the Gambino crime family was murdered as he was entering the restaurant, but most important is why he was there in the first place. It was probably for one of the gargantuan lobsters, ranging from 3 to 6 pounds, a perfectly crusted prime sirloin, aged in a combination of wet and dry aging techniques and a bottle or three from the endless wine list reputed to be one of the best in the city. Saturday nights are a bit calmer than weeknights, since a large part of the typical Sparks crowd is made up of suits abusing expense accounts.

Smith & Wollensky

797 3ʳᵈ Avenue, New York, NY 10022
(212) 753-1530

Danny Kissane, who has been in charge
of purchasing for Smith & Wollensky for
more than 30 years, selects only Prime
USDA beef for serving here. The beef
is then dry-aged in their technologically
futuristic dry aging chamber so that by
the time it gets to your plate 28 days
later, the meat has been tenderized and
enhanced in flavor like none other.
The wine cellar houses mostly American
wines, including their Private Reserves,
a Sauvignon Blanc and a Meritage,
perfect to pair with a steak or one of the
phenomenal surf and turf combinations.

Smith & Wollensky

Peter Luger

178 Broadway, New York, 11211
(718) 387-7400

Since 1887, this steakhouse right over
the Williamsburg Bridge has been taking
the steak game to higher heights, and
recently topped Zagat's list of steakhouses
for the 30ᵗʰ year in a row. It's no longer
a secret that they serve a burger at lunch
that rivals the best in the city. The menu,
much like the décor of the restaurant
(unadorned wood paneled walls and
plain butcher tables), is as straightforward
as you can get: Steak for one, steak for
two, steak for three and steak for four.
Keep in mind that Peter Luger is a cash
only operation.

Old Homestead

56 9th Avenue, New York, NY 10011
(212) 242-9040

The Old Homestead is the definitive old school Meatpacking District steakhouse. The steakhouse tradition has remained here since they first started grilling cuts of beef in 1868. The neighborhood outside has changed, and the menu has seen some as well (they were the first in the city to add Japanese Kobe beef to their menu), but none of this takes away from the pleasure of a perfectly charred NY Strip, served on a bare plate with nothing but a head of slow-roasted garlic that effortlessly spreads across the buttery tender meat.

NON TRADITIONAL STEAK HOUSES

Churrascaria Plataforma

316 West 49th Street, New York, NY 10019
(212) 245-0505

The Rodizio style restaurant offers a meat experience without equal. You're given a card, red on the one side and green on the other, and when you flip it to green, the waiters flock to your table, each bringing a different cut of meat on a skewer that they slice tableside. Throughout the night, up to twenty different kinds of meat may be offered. Included in the meal price is the appetizer buffet, filled with Brazilian staples like palmito and mandioca but also sushi and salads. Should you dare, there's also an option to add unlimited wine to the package.

Sammy's Roumanian

157 Chrystie Street, New York, NY 10002
(212) 673-0330

Walls covered in business cards and Polaroid's, and a ceiling with chipped paint that may or may not fall onto your table, it's still a destination for all New Yorkers looking to have a good time around a table covered in meat. Dani Luv, the resident DJ, has been injecting New York style into classic Jewish songs and you wouldn't be far off from thinking you'd walked into a bar mitzvah upon first entering the restaurant.

SPORTS

New York always has been and always will be a sports town, and no matter how bad any year might be for our teams, fans continue to shell out the big bucks to witness these multiple exercises in futility. The Knicks haven't won a championship since 1973, and that's a streak they look likely to continue for quite a while. The Mets somehow manage to find a new way to disappoint their fans every year, inevitably giving up all hopes of making the playoffs by the time the weather gets nice enough to go to the games. The Giants can go from winning a Super Bowl to not making the playoffs, and the Jets, well, best not to talk about the Jets. But New Yorkers are dreamers, and loyal, and with so many teams to choose from, the experience of attending a sporting event is still always high on the to do list.

Madison Square Garden, home of the Knicks and the Rangers, is one of the most storied buildings in the world, hosting not only 82 games a year between the basketball and hockey teams, but sold out concerts, boxing matches, and political conventions among other things over the years. The fact that it is located right in the heart of the city makes it all the more alluring. Nearly every night, throngs of fans in the blue and white colors of their teams surge out of the subway stations surrounding Penn Station, pre-gaming in the bars and taverns around the arena to ensure a healthy buzz before the first whistle. Walking into the Garden, decades of history photographed on the walls ignites the fervor, giving hope that perhaps tonight something will happen that can one day be immortalized on those walls.

On a beautiful spring day, or one of those summer nights when the heat is bearable, hopping a quick subway ride to one of the city's two major baseball stadiums can be a great way to spend the night. Whether you're headed to the Bronx to see the Yankees win or to Queens to see the Mets try to win, both Yankee Stadium and CitiField now offer a plethora of choices in the culinary department, along with fancy bars and lounges. But a hot dog and a beer while sitting in the bleachers is still the American pastime, and remains affordable to almost everyone.

New York's two football teams share a stadium across the river in Jersey, really just because housing an 80,000 person stadium in the city is still unimaginable. Every Sunday from September to

Madison Square Garden

CitiField

January, New Yorkers don their jerseys and beer helmets and migrate to the other side of the Hudson to roar at every touchdown and moan at every fumble. The $1.6 billion MetLife Stadium, where these games takes place, is the second biggest in the NFL in terms of seating capacity, and to hear those 80,000 plus people all cheer as one is an experience not to be missed.

Soccer has started to catch on in the States, and New York will soon be home to two teams. While the Red Bulls actually play across the river in New Jersey, NYCFC, the newest side project of Manchester City FC's wealthy Arab owners, joined the league in 2015 and is based in Queens. The stadiums are smaller and designed specifically for their teams, so with them filled to near capacity by dedicated fans at almost every match, the atmosphere is always spectacular and quite a welcome change from that of the sports Americans have traditionally grown up watching.

No matter what sport you love and what team drives you mad, whether you're from New York or your allegiances lie elsewhere, there's practically not a day of the year when you can't make your way to a beautiful stadium and let yourself go hoarse chanting or jeering as these amazing athletes try to bring another championship trophy home to New York.

SPORTS BARS

The definition of a sports bar has become quite blurry over the years: some are dedicated to specific sports or even specific teams, some are just regular neighborhood spots with enough televisions and drink specials to draw in the crowds, and some are part of a new high end trend that has taken the city by storm recently. But whether you're looking for a pint of Bud and some hot wings, craft beer and sliders or bottle service and gourmet plates while you watch your favorite team, there's definitely a bar out there for you to call home base.

Bounce Sporting Club

55 W 21st Street, New York, NY 10010
(212) 675-8007

Since sporting events end before the night should and the party must go on, Bounce Sporting Club in Chelsea has taken the precaution of making sure its upscale sports bar turns into a nightclub after the final whistle. Bottle service waitresses parade sparkler topped Champagne to red leather booths on one side of the place while attractive bartenders service the thirsty crowds at the long bar on the other. In the middle, everyone else angles for a view of the thirty or so televisions showing every sporting event imaginable. The menu classes up some old standards, serving hamburgers topped with Gruyere and a fried hen egg, duck sliders, and buttermilk fried chicken tenders to go along with buckets of domestic beer. But once the formalities are over, in house DJs take over the sound system and guarantee that nobody needs to head to any of the neighboring nightclubs.

Brother Jimmy's BBQ

Several locations throughout the city
www.brotherjimmys.com

Brother Jimmy's has been a destination for sports fans since 1989 when they first started pairing authentic southern BBQ with every sports package you care about. Delicious plates of ribs and pulled pork sandwiches along with various drink concoctions served in buckets, fishbowls and even "trash cans" make any Brother Jimmy's a worthy destination for sporting events. A good-looking staff wearing "Put Some South In Yo Mouth" t-shirts or cut off jerseys on game days adds to the festive atmosphere in this delicious BBQ joint. So when the Knicks are down twenty by the second quarter, you can always focus on your rib tips and which of Brother Jimmy's specialty sauces pairs best with them.

Brother Jimmy's BBQ

Nevada Smiths

Kettle of Fish

59 Christopher Street, Manhattan, NY 10014
(212) 414-2278

Kettle of Fish in the West Village has both the sophisticated charm you would expect from the neighborhood and an eclectic décor from the mind of a mad scientist. The 1950s looking subterranean lair, with a hearth, couches and board games, might not seem the typical sports bar, but come game time, the mix of cheap beer, darts and a great jukebox make this an ideal spot to watch any event with friends. Just keep in mind that come football Sunday, there's an obvious bias towards Packers fans, something you might've picked up on if you noticed all the cheese paraphernalia hanging around.

Nevada Smiths

100 3rd Avenue, New York, NY 10003
(212) 982-2591

Nevada Smith's is the football Mecca of New York City, showing over 100 live matches per week from around the world, meaning that yes, they open early in the morning for the big games. It's a good thing that drinks are served in plastic cups because across four floors, including two full bars, a VIP room and a separate wine bar, a little bit of hooliganry is the norm for the international fans that congregate here.

Mulholland's

312 Grand Street, Brooklyn, NY 11211
(718) 486-3473

On a busy strip in Brooklyn, Mullholland's stands out as an "IDIOT-FREE ZONE" (as a sign inside proclaims) to watch a game and enjoy a full menu that includes wings that come in flavors like Bloody Mary and Scorching Death. 12 HD flat screens, each labeled with the game it's showing so you can grab an appropriately positioned seat, ensure a pleasurable viewing experience while plush couches, a fireplace and a backyard patio will make you want to stay well past the final whistle.

OTHER OPTIONS

Village Pourhouse

64 3rd Avenue, New York, NY 10003
(212) 979-2337

The Ainsworth

122 W 26th St, New York, NY 10001
(212) 741-0645

The Royal

127 4th Avenue, New York, NY 10003
(212) 260-1099

Union Grounds

270 Smith St, Brooklyn, NY 11231
(347) 763-1935

JAPAN IN NYC

New York is home to a sizeable Japanese expat community and plenty of authentic restaurants to serve them. Alongside the seasoned masters of the sushi temples there are boisterous *izakayas, ramen dens* and *yakiniku* hotspots popping up all around town and begging for your chopsticks' attention. Whether you're craving raw fish delicacies straight from Japan's Tsujiki market, a humble bowl of Japanese noodles or an icy mug of *Sapporo* to go with some grilled *offal,* the ever-expanding Far East food scene can cater to your every wish.

15 East

15 East 15ᵗʰ Street, New York, NY 10003
(212) 647-0015

15 East is sleek downtown spot, with a very minimalist décor, that has a nine seat hubinga-wood sushi bar presided over by Masata Shimizu, formerly of Jewel Bako. Raw fish fanatics scheme to sit here and enjoy the master's stunning seafood preparations. Shimizu takes pleasure in educating novices and aficionados alike, occasionally pulling out various books and anatomy charts to show where his exceptional cuts of luscious, deep red tuna come from (a sampler of this fish with six different cuts is not to be passed up). The sushi at 15 East is punitively expensive, but it's definitely worth every dollar.

Geido

331 Flatbush Avenue, Brooklyn, NY 11217
(718) 638-8866

The great sushi masters haven't set up shop in Brooklyn, yet, but there is a reason why Geido, in Park Slope, has been drawing people in since 1985. Geido doesn't take itself too seriously: floor to ceiling graffiti, drawings of fish and caricatures of the staff cover the walls in this restaurant that those in the know say is as close as you can get to the feel of a neighborhood sushi joint in Tokyo. If you get to know chef/owner Osamu Koyama, the amount of sushi you get in the very reasonably priced *omakase* will vary depending on how much he has been drinking, and if he sees you appreciating his hard work, he won't hesitate to pour you a drink either.

Blue Ribbon Sushi

119 Sullivan Street, New York, NY 10012
(212) 343-0404

Though it's been open for more than a decade, until 2am no less, this beloved restaurant with a tavern like feel remains perennially jammed during peak hours. Not bound by tradition, but with a selection of flawless fish imported from around the world, the chefs are at their best when inventing interesting specials with the day's ingredients. Whether you go your own way with a few rolls and *nigiri* or with the chef's choice sushi platter, the ultra-fresh fish layered on perfectly cooked rice is something to remember. Don't leave before dessert, as the green-tea *crème brûlée* is a must.

Yasuda

204 East 43rd Street, New York, NY 10017
(212) 972-1001

Yasuda is still one of the tougher tables in town. Seat at the beautiful L-shaped bar where his longtime lieutenants, Tatsuya Sekiguchi and Mitsuru Tamura, elegantly serve purist renditions of nigiri onto wooden trays. Tatsu and Mitsu, as regulars like to call them, and their dedicated disciples, serve up bold offerings such as scallop roe or rock crab along with staples such as lightly seared and meltingly soft fatty tuna, all resting gently on lightly vinegar-moistened rice. You won't find elaborate combos here as the immaculate product is left to speak for itself.

Yasuda

Gyu-Kaku

Multiple locations
www.gyu-kaku.com

Gyu-Kaku is a great place to get acquainted with the Korean BBQ phenomenon. Once they light the grill at your table, it's easy to get into the idea of cooking your own meal in a restaurant. Platters of raw meat and fish come differently marinated and the staff lets you know how long to cook each piece. It's always best to come in groups as the set offerings give you more bang for your buck, and with a special happy hour from 9pm until close when dishes are half off and all the drinks are discounted, Gyu-Kaku is a great initiation into the world of *yakiniku*.

Totto Ramen

366 West 52nd Street, New York, NY 10019
(212) 582-0052

It's the golden age of ramen in New York at the moment, and crowds craving these satisfyingly rustic meals constantly mob Totto Ramen. Totto Ramen specializes in a Cantonese-influenced broth made with chicken and pork bones, along with soft, straight, or slightly wavy noodles, but the unique dish here is the *Paitan Ramen*, an uncommon style made with an opaque chicken stock that comes out creamy and intensely rich in texture and flavor. It's best to sit up-close at the counter and watch the cooks, their heads wrapped in black towels. There, you will also notice eggs marinating in a dark brown sake-soy liquid.

Gyu-Kaku

OYSTERS

"He was a bold man that ate the first oyster," Jonathan Swift once said. New York City is one of the best places in the world to enjoy fresh seafood, so whereas fried calamari can make for a great happy hour in more land-locked parts of the country, oysters rule the day when it comes to New York City. Some have to wait until five o'clock hits to run out of their offices and find the nearest raw bar while the lucky few can start earlier.

Essex

120 Essex Street, New York, 10002
(212) 533-9616

While Essex may be most famous for their brunch, their $1 oyster special, available all night long from Sunday through Thursday, is a great reason to keep coming back during the week. The selection may not be as varied as other places and the oysters tend to be on the smaller side, but long after other bars finish with happy hour, Essex keeps the party going until closing time and even offers half priced drinks from 5pm-8pm.

Crave Fishbar

945 2ⁿᵈ Avenue, New York, NY 10022
(646) 895-9585

With a new oyster bar located upstairs, Crave Fishbar in Midtown was bound to join the happy hour carnival. A dozen varieties of east and west coast oysters are all $1 each, including the west coasters normally priced at four times that, and drink specials run from $5 beers to half priced bottles of sparkling wine every weekday from

5pm-7pm. The raw bar also offers chilled shellfish such as jumbo lump crab meat and littleneck clams, and the selection of sauces brought to your table, including a delicious preserved lemon mignonette, ensure every slurpy mouthful will be a delight.

Docks Oyster Bar & Grill

633 3ʳᵈ Avenue, New York, NY 10017
(212) 986-8080

Whereas Essex goes late, Docks Oyster Bar & Grill is an early starter, offering $1 oysters from 3pm-7pm every weekday. A regular hangout for the city's financial players before they catch a train out of nearby Grand Central, a seat at the long wooden bar is ideal to enjoy any of a dozen varieties of expertly shucked oysters.

Fish

280 Bleecker Street, New York, NY 10014
(212) 727-2879

Bleecker Street may feel like a tourist trap, but tucked away right off of Jones Street you'll find Fish, where every night you can enjoy your choice of half a dozen oysters or clams with a PBR draft or glass of wine for only $8. That kind of deal is unbeatable in the city, and since the word is out, getting in early is a must if you want to enjoy the super fresh oysters in peace.

The John Dory Oyster Bar

1196 Broadway, New York, NY 10001
(212) 792-9000

The John Dory Oyster Bar has one of the best selections of seafood on the island. This spot is filled with a lively after work crowd that enjoys six oysters or clams with a glass of sparkling wine or a pint of Sixpoint Oyster Stout, a beer made from the oyster shells shucked right there in the restaurant, every weekday from 5pm-7pm. But The John Dory takes it one step farther by offering the special again from 11pm-midnight and on weekends from noon-7pm, when the deal can be paired with a *Bloody Mary* or *Michelada*.

Maison Premiere

298 Bedford Avenue, Brooklyn, NY 11211
(347) 335-0446

Maison Premiere is a charming Williamsburg oyster house that offers a happy hour from 4pm-7pm during the week and from 11am-1pm on weekends. There are over 30 types of oysters from around the country on the menu, and while there are no drink specials, the self proclaimed "oyster and cocktail den"

offers a wonderful selection of absinthe-based cocktails, along with wine.

Grand Central Oyster Bar

89 E 42ⁿᵈ Street, New York, NY 10017
(212) 490-6650

The grandfather of all oyster houses. Tucked into the lower level of Grand Central, the Grand Central Oyster Bar has been a destination for commuters, tourists and locals alike since 1913. Whether you choose the enormous main room filled with marble columns and long counters or prefer the wood-paneled saloon in the back, you'll find dozens of varieties of oyster, listed with helpful descriptors so that you can easily differentiate between *Naked Cowboys* and *Malpeques*, in a setting that alone is worthy of a visit.

Upstate

95 1ˢᵗ Avenue, New York, NY 10003
(917) 408-3395

At Upstate, a relative newcomer to the New York seafood scene located down near the beginning of First Avenue, a daily happy hour from 5pm-7pm offers six oysters and your choice of a craft beer or glass of wine for only $12. The oysters arrive fresh daily from both coasts and the drinks are all locally sourced. And no matter what you order, when the check arrives, it is always accompanied by a little slice of whisky-soaked pound cake to send you merrily on your way.

Grand Central Oyster Bar

Upstate

#

Buildings with ornate fire escapes, Corinthian columns and oversized windows, along with a skyline nearly devoid of skyscrapers, give this area south of Houston Street a charm that makes it one of the city's most beloved shopping and dining destination. For those that live north of 14th Street, an afternoon in Soho is practically a vacation, you could wander the cobblestone streets of Soho for hours filled with pleasure, but knowing where to stop makes the experience even better.

Soho is the original artists' neighborhood in New York. Since the 1970's it's been the epicenter of the avant-garde art world and the neighborhood offers all different kinds of experiences, as only on the corner of Prince Street and Broadway can you walk on a sidewalk carved by Keith Haring.

Artists Space

38 Greene Street #3, New York, 10012
(212) 226-3970

A very easy to miss contemporary art gallery hidden on the third floor of a nondescript building, once inside, a friendly staff is always on hand to provide explanations of the artists' motives, helping to make the artwork more accessible to the uninitiated.

Drawing Center

35 Wooster Street, New York, NY 10013
(212) 219-2166

As the name suggests, the Drawing Center is all drawing all the time, featuring first-rate exhibitions devoted to drawings and

works on paper, although some of the works blur the line between drawing and sculpture, making a short visit to this gallery a rather unique experience.

Soho Gallery For Digital Art

138 Sullivan Street, New York, NY 10012
(212) 228-2810

A digital art gallery and performance venue that showcases art from around the world. It usually attracts a younger crowd also eager to experience the presentations on the gallery's 16 40" screens located throughout the two-floor space. Named as one of the best contemporary art galleries in NYC, Soho Gallery for Digital Art has previously hosted *The International iPhoneography Show* as well as events for Instagram and FX Photo Studio.

Despite the arrival of Prada, Chanel, Dior Homme and Balenciaga creating a kind of Champs Elysées in Soho, the neighborhood remains a veritable playground for design and style aficionados.

Opening Ceremony

35 Howard Street, New York, NY 10013
(212) 219-2688

The concept is unique: every year a country is selected and both emerging designers and established brands from that country are presented. A great place to discover items you wouldn't find anywhere else.

American Two Shot

135 Grand St, New York, NY 10013
(212) 925-3403

Browsing indie-label offerings to designer clothing, you can grab an espresso and have fun all the way through the store to the photo-booth in the back. When it comes to trendy Soho boutiques, American Two Shot pretty much stands out.

Ina

101 Thompson Street, New York, NY 10012
(212) 941-4757

The store was made famous for acquiring the Sex in the City wardrobe when the show wrapped. The collections are one or two years old, and since most items come from photo shoots or runway shows the sizes tend to be on the smaller end of the spectrum, but all major brands are present and prices get slashed consistently until every consignment is sold.

After a day of shopping and gallery hopping, it's important to relax around some food and drink. To that end, Soho has more than its fair share of local favorites.

The Dutch

131 Sullivan Street, New York, NY 10012
(212) 677-6200

At night and during weekend brunch the restaurant is packed so taking advantage of the more laid back lunch hour is the perfect way to enjoy the eclectic menu, featuring standouts like the 18oz strip steak, the duck on rice, or the famous fried chicken, as well as an impressive list of cocktails.

Ed's Lobster Bar

222 Lafayette Street, New York, NY 10012
(212) 343-3236

Here lobster reigns supreme: you can enjoy it steamed, grilled, broiled, in ravioli and even in a pie. If you're looking to sit at one of the tables in the back, be prepared to wait, but whether you're stopping in for a quickie cocktail and *lobster roll* or a more substantial meal, the counter, with the raw bar options right in front of you, is a pleasant alternative.

Osteria Morini

218 Lafayette St, New York, NY 10012
(212) 965-8777

Michael White's homage to the classic Bolognese tavern, replete with burnt-orange terra-cotta façade and potted cypress trees outside the door. His seven years spent cooking in Italy's Emilia-Romagna region were all for the cause, as the *cappalletti*, pasta stuffed with truffled mascarpone, bathed in a butter sauce and then sprinkled with *prosciutto*, will attest. The wine list is less aggressively priced than at the other restaurants that make up his New York food empire, and simple, osteria-style desserts like the *panna cotta* are a perfect counterpoint to the impeccable but rich pasta dishes.

CENTRAL PARK

For New Yorkers, Manhattan alone deserves to be referred to as "the city" and it is in the same spirit that we refer to Central Park simply as "the park." Of course there are several parks in New York, but Central Park, covering nearly 850 acres in the middle of the island, is unparalleled in size and majesty. Extending from 59th Street to 110th Street, about 2.5 miles, the park contains lakes, baseball fields, zoos, theaters, playgrounds and many other things that allow us to forget the steel, concrete and glass of the outside world.

But Central Park is also like the city itself in that you learn to navigate through it according to time of day, mostly to avoid tourists and children, and every New Yorker probably has his favorite little secret spot somewhere in the park.

One of our favorite activities when the weather is favorable is a picnic in Central Park. When a picnic is announced, what may have been planned as an hour or two alone on the grass with a friend often rapidly morphs into a feast that lasts until sunset. And really, there aren't many places in New York better suited to see the sun: the park being one of the few places where you aren't oppressively surrounded by buildings, the open view allows you to fully appreciate the changing color of the sky and to see the sun go down between the buildings on the west side of Manhattan.

Sheep Meadow, around 68th Street on the west side of the park, is one of the most popular lawns for gatherings, but for good reason: a magnificent view of the skyscrapers along 59th Street, plenty of room to throw a frisbee, and even a small cafe adjacent that serves snacks.

Throughout the summer, there's non-stop music in Central Park. SummerStage always has big names from across all genres, with several of those concerts being free. They take place at Rumsey Playfield on the east side of the park, near the 72nd Street entrance, and though the shows often sell out quickly, don't worry, as sometimes it's even nicer to settle on the grass just outside and enjoy the music all the while avoiding the crowds inside.

The Great Lawn, a little further north, which during the day is full of athletes making use of the multiple baseball fields, in the evening, from time to time, hosts concerts on a completely different scale. In 2013, it hosted the Global Citizen Festival, a concert bringing together Stevie Wonder, Alicia Keys, John Mayer and others to raise awareness for poverty, and for those who prefer a bit of classical music, the

New York Philharmonic also plays for free in July to more than 50,000 listeners sitting under the stars.

Moving from music to theater, for more than fifty years now Shakespeare in the Park has been a favorite summer tradition for New Yorkers. These free performances take place at the outdoor Delacorte Theater, with the box office opening at noon the day of the performance. People line up hours in advance for the chance at a ticket to return the same evening to see, for example, someone like John Lithgow interpret King Lear.

One might think that Wolman Rink on the south side of the park is a trap solely for tourists, one of those places that New Yorkers would avoid like the plague, or Times Square, but every winter we come back, even if just once, for the majestic view of Manhattan's skyscrapers as we lap around the ice. The risk of having to share the ice with tourists and children is well worth it to enjoy a few spins with a special someone in such a romantic place.

Whether you're there for a walk along the paths, for a game of tennis, to visit the zoo with your family or to spend time with friends on the lake, Central Park is one of the few places in Manhattan where you can really take the time to get lost in the pleasures that make us forget city life.

LIVE MUSIC

The recording industry may be crumbling, but the city that brought you the Ramones, Beastie Boys, Blondie, Talking Heads and many others is still the best place in the country to discover new music. There's no feeling quite like thinking you've discovered a new band before they make it big, so from hole-in-the-wall dives where you can do just that to grand theaters where you can catch them later on in their careers, there's no shortage of places to rock out in this city. But sometimes, choosing how to spend your time and money is less about the performer than it is about the venue itself, as some offer a little more bang for the buck when it comes to acoustics, cheep drinks, vintage vibes and killer lineups. New Yorkers benefit from a cutthroat environment for musicians, and if you plan accordingly, on any given night you can catch more than one first-rate show in any of these following venues.

Bowery Ballroom

6 Delancey St, New York, NY 10002
(212) 533-2111

Converted from an old retail space on the Lower East Side in 1997, this intimate 550-person space has become famous for hosting one hip band after another and acting as a kind of intermediary between the pub gigs and the big stage.

Over three floors, with three bars, the venue is usually filled with a knowledgeable fan base of music fans on the cutting edge of what's new and hot, and with recent performers including the Pixies, Grizzly Bear Metric and Lauryn Hill, the vibe in the room may be a little bit on the hipster side but it's always a good time. As a bonus, the balconies are generally open to the public as opposed to a lot of places that reserve them for VIPs.

Rockwood Music Hall

196 Allen St, New York, NY 10002
(212) 477-4155

One of New York's favorite spots to experience future stars in the indie music scene. All the rooms are small and cozy (brick walls and burning candles in one for example), making amplification barely necessary as you're never too far from the strumming guitar. The schedule is filled with singer/songwriters that love to play here for the intimate vibe and phenomenal sound, and whether you are sitting down to enjoy a nice bottle of red (from a well thought out wine list that adds to the sophistication of the venue) or jamming out beer in hand to a rock band, if you brought a special friend with you, chances are she'll remember it as a great night.

Mercury Lounge

217 E Houston St, New York, NY 10002
(212) 260-4700

A favorite destination for rock stars and fans alike, and over the years has been the stage for artists like Lou Reed, Joan Jett and Jeff Buckley along with countless other stars who find the 250-person capacity lounge on the Lower East Side the perfect place to blur the lines between themselves and the audience. Even though up to four bands can rock out on any given night, the sound system has handled the abuse well and always produces impeccable sound. Separated from the performance area by soundproof doors, the bar in the front is ideal for grabbing a drink with friends while you wait for your band to take the stage.

Beacon Theater

2124 Broadway, New York, NY 10023
(212) 465-6500

The 3,000-person capacity Beacon Theater on the Upper West Side underwent a $16 million renovation a few years back. With a new sound system in place, the acoustics here are first rate, and there is not one obstructed sightline in the venue. The bands tend to cater to an older crowd – aside from the Allman Brothers who have been playing here for decades you might catch Sting, Simply Red or Sade - but the marriage of classic rock and old world Art Deco design make for an unforgettable show.

Music Hall Of Williamsburg

66 N 6ᵗʰ St, Brooklyn, NY 11211
(718) 486-5400

A mid-sized venue just one subway stop from Manhattan, the Music Hall of Williamsburg often hosts secret shows for bands who have sold out bigger venues like Webster Hall. Top shelf artists such as Phoenix, LCD Soundsystem and Delorean have played here, and in 2009 John Mayer played a secret show here before his performance at the Beacon Theater. It's often referred to as the younger brother of the Bowery Ballroom due to its similar layout, and while shows are occasionally oversold here, the multitude of vantage points allay the need to push to the front.

Webster Hall

125 E 11ᵗʰ St, New York, NY 10003
(212) 353-1600

Webster Hall is the biggest music club in New York City, and since it's inception back in 1896, this multilevel space has effortlessly vacillated from dance hall to live music venue and from hip-hop hangout to salsa palace. In rooms such as the Marlin Room, the Studio and the Grand Ballroom, you can see acts ranging from Kings Of Leon to various hip-hop groups and DJ's and the many distinct environments, types of music, and people that flock to this venue constantly transform Webster Hall into an ever-changing, four-story funhouse.

JAZZ CLUBS

New York City has always claimed bragging rights as the jazz capital of the world, but in recent years, New York jazz has resurged in a special way. Independent labels and festivals are restoring the music's status from respectably classy to refreshingly hip. Although many of the pioneering joints like Cotton Club, Lenox Lounge and the original Birdland where the genre developed and evolved have since been shuttered, there are still plenty of clubs around town where you can go to immerse yourself in the real stuff.

Blue Note Jazz Club

131 West 3rd Street, New York, NY 10012
(212) 475-8592

An institution, where musical titans such as Dizzie Gillespie, Chick Corea and Sarah Vaughan play the same stage. The Friday and Saturday night "Late Night Groove Series," with only an $8 cover charge, attracts a younger crowd that has a real feel for the independent music scene. The close-set tables in the club get patrons rubbing up against each other, making for a convivial atmosphere, and on any given night, it's nothing out of the ordinary to see a musical legend seated in the audience get called up on stage for a little jam.

Iridium Jazz Club

1650 Broadway, New York, NY 10019
(212) 582-2121

Iridium is known to many jazz aficionados as the New York City home of the late, great Les Paul. For more than 12 years, the legendary musician played weekly performances here and now they honor his legacy with Les Paul Mondays. The stage is designed to be close to the public and the acoustics are wonderful, making it a friendly place where jazz lovers can take in sets played by some of the best-known names in the business. The only real drawback to this club is that it's in Times Square, a part of town loathed because of the insane tourist action, but once in a while it's worth braving it to be in a place where artists such as Jacky Terrasson, The Jazz Messengers and Clark Terry all recorded live sets.

Smalls Jazz Club

183 W 10th Street, New York, NY 10014
(212) 252-5091

For those looking for an authentic jazz club experience, Smalls is a must. There was a time when a $10 cover charge would get you into this dark little cave down some stairs on West 10th Street where you could sit back to hear some legendary musicians like Joshua Redman, Brad Mehldau, Norah Jones, Kurt Rosenwinkel and Roy Hargrove. Though the cover charge has now doubled, the raw energy of the tiny 48 seat room survives. Unlike most clubs, the music plays on until 4am every night of the week. If you hang out long enough, eventually a seat will free up.

Smoke Jazz & Supper Club Lounge

2751 Broadway, New York, NY 10025
(212) 864-6662

Opened in 1999, Smoke has developed into a hip and casually swank jazz joint with enough chops and personalities to recommend it to serious fans of NY jazz. Low-lit chandeliers, comfy sofas, plush carpeting and unobstructed sight lines make it seem like the greats are playing in your living room. When it comes to the menu, Smoke is a step up

Smoke Jazz & Supper Club Lounge

from some of its compatriots, so lovers of fried chicken and smooth jazz 'n blues can't do much better than this. Smoke has hosted the likes of George Coleman and Bill Charlap in the past, Trumpeter Wynton Marsalis is a regular, and fleet-fingered pianist Bill Charlap once played four sold-out sets accompanied by Ron Carter and Kenny Washington. There are themed nights throughout the week, such as Latin Jazz on Sundays, but on Fridays and Saturdays, famous locals like Eddie Henderson and Cedar Walton hit the stage.

Village Vanguard

178 7ᵗʰ Avenue South, New York, NY 10014
(212) 255-4037

This 80-year-old temple to jazz is arguably the most famous venue in the history of the music. The full list of performers who have graced the stage is simply an encyclopedia of the top names in jazz, including Thelonius Monk, Miles Davis and Cecil Taylor and extending through today's biggest names. Not the best looking club in the city, in fact, the staircase leading to the basement is dangerously steep and the green basement itself quite ragged looking, but the brilliant acoustics of the room have enabled it to serve as a recording studio for artists such as Sonny Rollins and Wynton Marsalis. And this place really is all about the music. In fact, they don't even serve food, because really, the music is the only reason you're here.

Barbès

376 9ᵗʰ Street, New York, NY 11215
(347) 422-0248

Barbès is an intimate spot located in south Park Slope that will impress even the snobbiest and most claustrophobic of jazz fans. There's usually no cover charge, although a $10 donation is suggested, definitely making it one of the cheapest options when it comes to catching some good live music. In addition to jazz, they've also got lots of global music, like the mighty Slavic Soul.

DESSERT SPOTS

By now, the whole world has heard of New York's insane cronut craze and the comical lengths that people go to in order to get their hands on one, but to focus on that one pastry is a shame when there's an entire city filled with bakeries doing wonderful things that are terrible for you. New Yorkers take dessert seriously, and regardless of how hard the anti-obesity campaigns are assailing the public, there are fantastic bake shops, boulangeries and pasticcerias to keep New Yorkers satisfied. Life without dessert is a terrible thing, and these places are here to make sure none of us have to suffer too long in between sugar highs.

Dominique Ansel Bakery

189 Spring Street, New York, NY 10012
(212) 219-2773

The aforementioned *cronut*, a deep-fried, cream-filled croissant/donut hybrid, is good. It's actually really ridiculously good, but it's not what you should be waiting on line for at Dominique Ansel Bakery. Ansel, who before opening his own shop was the executive pastry chef at Daniel Boulud's flagship restaurant, has been topping the lists of best bakeries since his opening, mainly thanks to his Dominique's Kouign Amann, the "DKA", a caramelized croissant with a crispy shell and a flaky interior that was voted one of Time Out New York's best dishes of 2012. The brilliant pastry chef is constantly impressing the public with new inventions, from chocolate chip cookies shaped like shot glasses and filled with cold milk to the Paris-NY, a twist on the Paris-Brest that has a choux dough and a chocolate, caramel and peanut butter filling.

Two Little Red Hens

1652 2ⁿᵈ Avenue, New York, NY 10028
(212) 452-0476

In the pantheon of iconic New York foods, not much outranks the cheesecake. The cheesecake is a dessert that's perfect in its simplicity. A silky, creamy base, an optional thin crust—and that's it. Sky-high, smooth and slightly tart, the cheesecake at Two Little Red Hens has become a neighborhood and citywide favorite. A browned top gives way to a thick, rich filling, which sits on a heavenly graham cracker crust. The cheesecake takes 24 hours to set so there are usually no slices available on Monday or Tuesday mornings. But whole cheesecakes are available all week, with prices ranging from $27 for a cake that feeds 6 to $54 for 32, which certainly seems expensive until you've actually tasted one. That's when you really understand the price of decadence. The Upper East Side stalwart is also known for their selection of seasonal pies and fruit-studded tarts.

Two Little Red Hens

Lady M Confections

41 East 78ᵗʰ Street, New York, NY 10075
(212) 452-2222

Since 2001 Lady M has been conquering the hearts, eyes and stomachs of all who've tried the splendid desserts at the pristine and elegant white walled boutique.
The display of French and Japanese pastries is so masterfully presented you're almost scared to slice into the cakes for fear of damaging their idyllic nature. The legendary *Mille Crêpe Cake*, a glorious creation made of at least twenty thin handmade crêpes lathered in between with airy velvety pastry cream, has become such a phenomenon that it has led Lady M to open outposts in Los Angeles and Singapore as well.

Momofuku Milk Bar

251 East 13ᵗʰ Street, New York, NY 10003
(347) 577-9504

The must-try walk-up dessert shop that is a part of David Chang's Momofuku empire. One of the real draws is the salty pistachio soft serve ice cream. The Electro Freeze soft serve machines in place at Milk Bar had to be customized to accommodate flavors like this, and whatever they had to do was worth it: it tastes like the smoothest and creamiest freshly roasted and salted pistachio gelato you can imagine, only it's soft serve. The flavored milks and *crack pie* (no crack, just butter, heavy cream, brown sugar, sugar and a little corn flour) are also perfect for a post dinner sweet treat.

Sugar Sweet Sunshine

126 Rivington Street, New York, NY 10002
(212) 995-1960

Perhaps one of the least pretentious bakeries in New York. Decorated with funky light fixtures and mismatched thrift-shop furniture, it's the kind of joint whose retro appeal reliably allures, regardless of what's for sale. And what's for sale is cupcakes, in fun flavors like "Sunshine" (yellow cake with vanilla buttercream) or "Bob" (yellow cake with chocolate almond buttercream). They cost about 2 bucks each and take a kind of anti-patisserie approach where taste counts more than looks. One bite in and all your worries will disappear.

Baked

359 Van Brunt Street, Brooklyn, New York 11231
(718) 222-0345

This little Red Hook bakeshop originally made waves with its signature *Sweet & Salty Brownie*, which earned high praise from the likes of Martha Stewart.
It's not the only item worth scoping out. Tourists and locals alike make their way to this popular Red Hook spot for *Chunkwiches*—ice cream sandwiched between thick, homemade cookies— the thick, gooey *cloud cookies* and their *Millionaire Bars*, made with caramel, chocolate and short bread. You can wash it all down with a steaming cup of espresso or indulge in the bakery's velvety hot chocolate.

WINE STORES

We live in a world today where virtually anything can be ordered online at any time and delivered directly to your doorstep, including wine and spirits. While that facility can be excused in some instances, it should not discourage people from frequenting and supporting our neighborhood merchants. No matter what part of the city you're in, you can find a nearby a store with an educated and approachable staff. We've come a long way since stereotyping wine as a thing for the rich and pretentious, and New York's best wine stores all provide a wonderful and welcoming experience.

Appellation Wine & Spirits

156 10th Avenue # 1, New York, NY 10011
(212) 741-9474

Since 2005, Scott Pactor, has been stocking the city's best selections of organic, biodynamic and sustainable wines at Appellation Wines & Spirits. Because the natural wine market is relatively unknown to the average consumer, there is a lot of face-to-face time with the staff, and often, in the evenings, Pactor will open a select bottle and lead a tasting himself. Bolstering his commitment to wine education, there is a bookshelf filled with books on viniculture and cooking, making this a place to visit for more than just a quick purchase.

Crush Wine & Spirits

153 E 57th St, New York, NY 10022
(212) 980-9463

Crush could be a museum for wine. In a beautiful location on 57th Street,

the expansive collection of wine is displayed in a temperature-controlled space, the bottles neatly stacked on their sides, as they should be but often aren't elsewhere. There is a special room dedicated to high-end selections and rare vintages, but Crush also stocks a fantastic selection of wines under $20, and with certified sommeliers on staff to advise, anyone can walk in and walk out with the perfect recommendation. Additionally, Crush houses one of the best collections of fortified wines in the city so amateurs of port, sherry and Madeira will not be disappointed.

Le Dû's Wines

600 Washington St, New York, NY 10014
(212) 924-6999

Jean-Luc Le Dû was the sommelier at Restaurant Daniel when he decided to open his eponymous store in the West Village back in 2005. His team travels the world tasting wines and bringing back unknown varieties, presenting a small but one-of-a-kind selection of bottles in the store. You'll find amazing wines from $10 to $200, and much higher if you so desire, but what really sets Le Dû's Wine & Spirits apart are the epic tastings that Jean-Luc hosts at which he's been known to open rather expensive bottles from time to time. People from all over Manhattan make the trip to Le Dû's specifically to take classes in the temperature-controlled back room, but if you happen to be in the neighborhood at all, it's always worth a little visit.

Pasanella & Sons

115 South St, New York, NY 10038
(212) 233-8383

Pasanella & Sons is the pet project of a husband and wife team who live above the wine store down on South Street. This charming shop has French doors that open up into a small back garden where tastings, classes and private events are held. The store itself arranges its wines by the type of food you would eat with it, such as pizza, or barbecue, and the piece de resistance is a '64 Fiat Giardiniera station wagon that houses the rosé selections. Pasanella & Sons subscribes to the same philosophy of presenting New Yorkers with under the radar wines, with some of its 400-plus bottle selection of artisanal wines and accessories grouped into themed packages such as "Just Got A Raise" or "The Basic Bar."

Sherry-Lehmann Wine & Spirits

505 Park Avenue, New York, NY 10022
(212) 838-7500

Sherry-Lehmann is the granddaddy of wine stores in New York, it is the headquarters of French wine in New York and is widely recognized as having the best selection of wines in the country. The mind-blowing catalog, which features over 7,000 different bottles, is only partially on display, but with one of the best websites in the business, if you find what you want and order it online, their shuttle will have it delivered to the store before you know it.

UVA Wines

199 Bedford Avenue, NY 11211
(718) 963-3939

When I find myself in Brooklyn and in need of a bottle of wine to bring somewhere, Uva is always the destination of choice. The store somehow manages to pack 300 bottles of wine into a 500 square foot space, many of them elegantly displayed on tilted racks at eye level. France and Italy are the most represented countries at Uva, and about one third of the wines on hand cost less than $12. Green dots throughout the store identify organic and biodynamic wines, and the staff members, who taste nearly every bottle on sale, are always willing and eager to explain the differences between the grapes on hand.

Pasanella & Sons

WINE BARS

Eclipsed these last few years by the vogue of the cocktail den, wine bars are now enjoying a second coming thanks to funky and affordable lists that attract oenophiles searching for new experiences as well as novices seeking to be initiated. The ambiance is often intimate and appealing, the service personal and the food simple. Whereas wine bars used to focus on Italian wine and food pairings, today's most popular destinations offer wines from France, South Africa, Chile and elsewhere, along with a fine selection of organic wines.

D.O.C. Wine Bar

83 North 7th Street, Brooklyn, NY 11211
(718) 963-1925

Williamsburg didn't get left behind when it comes to rustic Italian wine bars, and stepping into D.O.C. actually feels like teleporting to a fairytale Sardinian cottage. A largely Italian crowd gathers until late into the night to raucously toast each other with glasses of vintage selections from Sicily or Campania, while the menu emphasizes Sardinian meats and sheep's milk cheeses.

Aroma Kitchen & Wine Bar

36 E 4th Street, New York, NY 10003
(212) 375-0100

From what used to be a clothing store, owners Alexandra Degiorgio and Vito Polosa have created Aroma, a cozy little wine bar in the East Village that oozes simplistic charm. The moment you walk in you see shelves filled with wine on the exposed brick walls, a long bar carved out of a single tree trunk and crystal chandeliers providing dim lighting to make for quite the rustic atmosphere. The kitchen serves more than just bar snacks and on Monday's even offers a five course tasting menu, but the wine selection is really the main attraction, one worth making this place a stop anytime you're in the area.

Vero

1483 2nd Avenue, New York, NY 10021
(212) 452-3354

Vero is not just your typical Upper East Side date spot. It's the kind of place where people from the neighborhood meet up and where those who come in for the first time are immediately made to feel like part of the family. Just make your way passed the few tables at the terrace and you'll enter a tiny space with

City Winery

Vero

a bar leading back to the dining area's twelve tables and ending with a miniscule open kitchen. It may be small, but it is effective: succulent meatballs resting in a bowl of spicy tomato sauce, an exquisite tuna tartare, and Vero's famous *paninis* (complimentary with the purchase of a drink on Mondays). Wines are offered by the bottle or by the glass, but also, for the undecided or uninitiated, in tasting flights, a selection of several smaller glasses to help the novice find his pleasure.

City Winery

155 Varick Street, New York, NY 10013
(212) 608-0555

This 21,000 square foot space includes a wine bar, a cheese bar, a wine focused restaurant and a stage for music. The rustic space evokes a laid back California vineyard feeling that enhances the wine tasting experience. If you're willing to break the piggybank, you can have your own barrel in the basement with a wine you personally craft from grape to bottle. For the rest, a well-structured wine list offers several glasses for less than $10. Here, the food accompanies the wine, not the other way around, and the waiters take your wine order before proposing suggested pairings.

The Ten Bells

247 Broome Street, New York, NY 10002
(212) 228-4450

The Ten Bells, named after the bar where Jack the Ripper would meet his victims, doesn't look like your typical wine bar. This dark, small (30 seats) place only serves wines from small organic producers from the likes of Europe, Oregon and Morocco. You would need a magnifying glass to make out the wine list detailed on the chalkboards, but that's a good thing as it opens you up to suggestions from a staff that really knows the cult wines from these regions. Small plates such as oysters, *charcuterie* from Basque country or classic tapas, such as *patatas bravas*, are the perfect accompaniment in a place where the ambiance encourages you to hang loose and wile away the hours.

Peasant

194 Elizabeth Street, New York, NY 10012
(212) 965-9511

Located in the basement of the eponymous restaurant, Peasant is an enoteca that offers everything you could ask for from an Italian wine bar: a wine cellar, stone pillars, exposed beams, brick walls, communal tables, flickering candles and hearty meat and cheese plates. The wine bottle list changes weekly, but always remains affordable, and pairs well with the salumi offerings and imported cheeses provided by nearby specialty store DiPaolo's. This distinctly European wine cellar is ideal for more laid back get-togethers.

NIGHTCLUBS

Despite much of the city becoming a playground for tourist families from around the world, when we're looking for a fun night out, New York is filled with the delirium we all seek. With dance music riding an unparalleled wave of popularity, the resurgence of the dance club means that when you and your friends are looking for a party with good music and hoping to meet someone to keep the party going on with later, your options are nearly infinite. The landscape of New York City nightclubs is ever changing, but as of now, these are the places you want to be.

Cielo

18 Little West 12th Street, New York, NY 10014
(212) 645-5700

Located in the heart of the Meatpacking District, Cielo is a smaller, more intimate dance club (about 300 people) that offers a self-proclaimed "mature" experience focused more on music and dancing than VIP bottle service. Though it's armed with one of the world's best sound systems and a specially designed sunken dance floor bathed in an extensive lighting system. New York old-schoolers like Francois K and Tedd Patterson run the scene here but big name DJs routinely come in for blowout parties.

Finale

199 Bowery, New York, NY 10002
(212) 980-3011

A Lower East Side den of decadence designed to deliver a high energy experience. Blue tufted walls and banquettes line the club, a rosewood bar accented with polished chrome anchors the space, a video wall behind the DJ provides an interesting touch and a ribbon of LED lights crowning the dance floor adds to the frenzy. *Tuesday Baby Tuesday*, New York's longest lasting weekly party, consistently draws a top notch crowd to Finale, and international headliners occasionally play here, so table reservations are recommended to ensure smooth entry.

Le Bain

848 Washington Street, New York, NY 10014
(212) 645-4646

The Standard Hotel's penthouse houses Le Bain, a nightclub with spectacular views of Manhattan and the Hudson River and the only swimming pool on a dance floor in the city (vending machines in the bathroom sell bathing suits for the unprepared). The musical programming is less mainstream than in most places, the door is not as exclusive as it once was, especially if you arrive before midnight with at least as many girls as guys, and when you need a breather, you can head upstairs to one of New York's most spacious rooftops, complete with a crepe stand.

Le Baron

32 Mulberry St, New York, NY 10013
(212) 962-2545

When you step inside Andre Saraiva's boutique, you're instantly transported into another world. The three floors are all filled with an experienced nightlife crowd of successful fashion forward creative types and beautiful women draped in black. Pop music from the 80s and 90s and some hip hop plays upstairs while the lower level is reserved for deep house and other electronic genres. If you know about Le Baron, you know about the tight door policy, but if you have the right image and are in a small group, you'll have a chance of getting in.

Southside

2 Cleveland Place, New York, NY 10013
(212) 680-5601

One of Soho's only late night options to pack the checkered dance floor and let loose. A nearly $300,000 sound system plays soul, house, and electro (strictly no hip hop) to a max crowd of about 200. There are a few leather booths to sit and enjoy a cocktail, but the high energy of the place is a direct result of the fact that people really do come here to have a good time dancing. Southside is definitely bearing the load in helping to revive the underground NYC dance party.

Output

74 Wythe Avenue, New York, NY 11211
(917) 333-1000

Output is not your conventional nightclub. No VIP guest lists, no bottle service and no cameras, Output is for any and all who value the communal experience of music over taking selfies in the club. It feels more like a permanent warehouse party than a New York City nightclub. It's been hailed as the savior of the city's nightlife and has "Perfect sound, amazing lineups and great Sunday parties," according to Seth Troxler, who adds, "If you want underground music, there is nowhere better in America."

Bespoke Musik

soundcloud.com/bespoke-musik
www.facebook.com/bespokemusik

An all-in-one company best known for underground warehouse events in Brooklyn and summertime boat parties, which have featured artists such as Dan Ghenacia, Andhim, Daniel Bortz, Rampue, & Stavroz as well as an internationally renown radio show on Soundcloud. Their parties are becoming increasingly legendary in the city, and should you be in the city for one of their summer boat parties, it's a no-brainer must-do.

Output

Bespoke Musik

A TRIP TO FRANCE

For a while towards the end of the 20th century, all of the most highly celebrated restaurants in the city were French. By the turn of the century though, this all began to feel quite outmoded, and the emphasis turned towards redefining American classics and exotic fusions. But after a decade of high-end burgers and fancy noodle dishes dominating the scene, a new era of classic cooking and good wine is coming back into style. France is once again en vogue, and the French are back to remind New Yorkers that they still run the show when it comes to romancing with food and drink.

Cercle Rouge

241 W Broadway, New York, NY 10013
(212) 226-6252

Cercle Rouge resonates with the nostalgia of Paris and the sophistication of TriBeCa. Its style emulates the 1970 movie of the same name: tiled floors, aged mirrors, vintage posters covering cream-colored walls and just enough red to entice the eye. Chef Pierre Landet sticks to Gallic staples like a steak frites so tender you don't need a knife and a duck breast smothered in cassis sauce accompanied by a fresh mushroom gratin, while a raw bar in the back covers the seafood spectrum from caviar to oysters. On July 14, Cercle Rouge celebrates by shutting down the street and setting up 18 sand covered pétanque courts with 62 teams competing while merguez sandwiches and Ricard and Lillet drinks are on sale for the spectators. Music and can-can dancers complete the festive atmosphere.

Lafayette

380 Lafayette St, New York, NY 10012
(212) 533-3000

Lafayette is a massive restaurant you get to after passing through the bakery and the rotisserie. The restaurant itself, with its tiled columns and giant windows, is filled with cushy booths as far as the eye can see, constantly packed, like the amber-lit bar past the bakery, with beautiful people. Fresh oysters, duck au poivre, Moroccan spiced lamb chops, tartare, handmade pastas, steak frites, bouillabaisse, rotisserie chicken for two and an apple tart for two… the options here are endless. Every Monday night, Lafayette serves a four-course prix fixe menu with dishes from one specific region of France. And just in case the main areas are over crowded, downstairs, a rustic brick wine cellar has its own bar.

Orsay

1057 Lexington Avenue, New York, NY 10021
(212) 517-6400

The type of restaurant you would eat at three or four times a week if you had the means. Designer Jean Denoyer's combination of Art Nouveau-style ceiling molding, wood paneling and chandeliers is both sophisticated and welcoming, as is the menu of mostly classic French dishes (perfectly cooked steak frites, braised lamb shank, raw bar) and a few pleasant twists, like the Japanese inspired tuna tartare prepared with a hint of wasabi, sesame and tempura. The award-winning wine list, which includes 225 predominantly French and American varietals, is tempting enough to saddle up to the zinc bar or grab a table on the terrace when the weather permits.

Café Gitane

242 Mott Street, New York, NY 10012
(646) 334-9552

Café Gitane was one of the first upscale spots to hit Nolita in the 90's. And yet, 20 years later, for those willing to brave the line of models, designers, shoppers and tourists waiting for a table, Café Gitane is still serving French-Moroccan dishes like herbed goat cheese with chili flakes and pomegranate syrup or spicy meatballs in a tumeric tomato sauce with boiled egg, cucumber-yogurt and cilantro. The tiny dining room gets packed and noisy, but all the action really takes place under the cloud of cigarette smoke that hides the few tables out front.

Artisanal Fromagerie Bistro and Wine Bar

2 Park Avenue, New York, NY 10016
(212) 725-8585

A shrine to cheese, the passion of chef-owner Terrance Brennan. After an olfactory assault at the door by the aroma of the nearly 200 varieties of cheese, gastronomes marvel over the restaurant's four different famous *fondues* (the Manchego & Chorizo, a perennial favorite) and other cheese imbued fare, like the addictive *gougère* cheese puffs and the onion soup *gratiné*. For those not so cheese-obsessed, there's a full menu of bistro classics like *boudin blanc, steak frites* and oysters. As well as a selection of over 150 wines by the glass.

Le Barricou

533 Grand Street, Brooklyn, NY 11211
(718) 782-7372

A gorgeous bistro boasting an elegant bar, a romantic back room and a library, the combination of which brings a rustic countryside ambiance to an unassuming stretch of Grand Street in Brooklyn. The second the temperature dips below 50, the management gets the old cast-iron fireplace stoked with logs, fire the perfect companion for affordable classics like *cassoulet, bouillabaisse* and *coq au vin.* Even the burger, a juicy piece of Pat LaFrieda beef served on a buttery *brioche* accompanied by delicious *frites* feels French.

BEER GARDENS

New York may be an urban jungle, but that doesn't mean we don't have spacious gardens perfect for kicking back in Bavarian style, and when the summer sunshine brings on a thirst that only a huge frosty stein can quench, all it takes is an open air area, picnic-style tables and imported brews to get the party going. From the classic biergarten that maintains old world traditions in the new world to newer incarnations that blur the true definition, good weather in New York means leaving the dusty dive bar behind and spending a light hearted afternoon raising a glass in the garden.

Hofbräu Bierhaus NYC

712 3rd Avenue, New York, NY 10017
(646) 580-2437

Hofbrau Bierhaus is a German restaurant located around the corner from Grand Central Station that serves up all the traditional favorites, from smoked trout filet to sauerkraut balls and gravlax to goulash. In addition to the menu, Bierhaus has 24 beers on tap, including six varieties of Hofbrau beer. The beer hall occupies the sky-lit upper floor of a two-story building, outfitted with long communal tables, blue-and-white Bavarian pennants and a 50-foot balcony overlooking 3rd Avenue. It may be one of the newest additions to the beer garden craze, but it has already developed quite the following among German foodies and on Thursday and Friday evenings, a German-American band called Alpine Squeeze helps set the festive drinking mood.

La Birreria

200 5th Avenue, New York, NY 10010
(212) 937-8910

Just because they're Italian doesn't mean they don't know anything about brewing beer. La Birreira is the sleek, contemporary take on the beer garden craze, as imagined by Mario Batali and Joe Bastianich of Eataly. During the colder months, the 4,500sf bar is a cozy greenhouse, but as the weather warms, the panes of glass open to reveal spectacular views. Though there are a few options, as the name would indicate, the emphasis is not on German food here. On this roof deck, you'll marry your unfiltered, unpasteurized, naturally carbonated cask ales brewed right on the premises with Italian favorites like blood sausage sandwiches or fried shitake mushrooms all the while taking in glorious views of the Flatiron and the Empire State Building.

Harlem Tavern

2153 Frederick Douglass Boulevard, New York, NY 10026, (212) 866-4500

Harlem Tavern has an open space out front that can seat nearly 300 people at its communal and bistro tables as well as an indoor area filled with people watching sporting events on television or listening to live jazz. The bar offers 20 drafts, like Ommegang and Lagunitas, and 25 bottles, some with inventive names like Flying Dog Raging Bitch and Cony Island Albino Python. From the kitchen flow a variety of entrées and snacks that can soak up the suds, such as the fried green tomato flatbread or the spicy gumbo, perfect to devour as you enjoy the view of Frederick Douglass Boulevard and think back on the history of this neighborhood.

Loreley

7 Rivington Street, New York, NY 10002 (212) 253-7077

While many beer gardens take their cue from Bavaria, Lorely is inspired by the

Loreley

German city of Cologne, and though they serve up German comfort food, like stacked plates of grilled and charred bratwurst from Schaller & Weber and potato pancakes with apple sauce, and keep 12 German beers on tap, that's where tradition ends. There's no folk music and no waitresses in dirndls here. The bar has a laid back appeal, with exposed brick walls, a skylight and handcrafted picnic tables, and it attracts a chill neighborhood crowd that sips giant mugs of lager like Spaten Ur-Märzen or any of the other international brews on tap.

Loreley

Zum Schneider

107 Avenue C, New York, NY 10009
(212) 598-1098

Opened by Bavaria native Sylvester Schneider in 2000, Zum Schneider is an ode to the summers he spent there when he was growing up. His dream of bringing an authentic beer garden to Alphabet City has been realized, with a restaurant that is especially well known for its Oktoberfest and World Cup parties. Schneider keeps 12 German beers on tap, and the menu features traditional Bavarian-German food, with seasonal specialties. Setting it apart from most beer gardens is a respectable wine list.

Radegast Hall & Biergarten

113 North 3rd Street, New York, NY 11211
(718) 963-3973

If you want to chug lagers like Weihenstephaner Dunkel Weisse or Pilsner Urquel in mugs that question both your sanity and sobriety level, there's an authentic German bierhalle in Williamsburg waiting for you. If you're seated at one of the massive communal 150-year-old bard wood tables outside under the retractable roof, forget the menu and head to the grill. There you'll find sizzling brats and Polish sausages that you'll order just as an excuse to keep eating their addictive mustard. Just about every night features live music, including live jazz on Wednesdays and Thursdays.

BARBERSHOPS

Women in New York are spoiled with an abundance of excellent hair salons, but for a man, finding a barber can quickly become an anxiety inducing mission, especially in a city like ours where if you don't watch out, you could just as easily overpay as get nicked by a blade, or, worst of all, walk out wearing a hat so nobody sees what happened to your head. New York is filled with independent barbershops that have a range of styles, services, prices, and, most importantly, drink offerings. Male grooming should be a pleasure, and it's one that these businesses specialize in providing.

Barbiere NYC

246 East 5th Street, New York, NY 10003
(646) 649-2640

Lello Guida grew up in his father's barbershop in Naples (the one in Italy), watching his old man practice the craft he would later master, opening shops of his own there before making the move to NYC. You won't catch anyone using clippers to cut hair in Lello's charming carriage house turned barbershop in the East Village, and a shave here is a multi step process that includes eucalyptus scented towels and ends with a an application of Moroccan rhassol clay, a refreshing treatment for dry skin. To up the relaxation ante, each shave comes with a complimentary shot of whiskey. Just know that a cut will set you back $40, and pairing it with a shave will run you $70.

The Blind Barber

339 East 10th Street, New York, NY 10009
(212) 228-2123

Although the Blind Barber has become famous for the speakeasy located in the back, the unassuming barbershop in front still provides a great service. True, the prices aren't cheap ($40 for a cut, $30 for a shave with their house-made shaving cream), but each of their services is accompanied by a cocktail made on the premises. In fact, as soon as you're done in the chair, you'll be invited through a door in the back that opens up into a 1920's speakeasy style bar, perfect for showing off your new look while sipping on a variety of spirits, including the Blind Barber's signature cocktail, the Sweeney Todd.

Frank's Chop Shop

Frank's Chop Shop

19 Essex Street, New York, NY 10002
(212) 228-7442

Frank's is an appointment only barbershop on the Lower East Side that's been servicing the neighborhood's trendy residents for years. Don't let the appointment-only policy turn you off, because all it means is you not having to wait for your cut ($30 for a traditional cut, or, for the more adventurous, a custom design carved into your mane will cost you $60). A quartet of comfortable 1930's style barber chairs is where the action takes place, and a great musical selection plays continuously to set a vibrant mood.

Freeman's Sporting Club

8 Rivington Street, New York, NY 10002
(212) 673-3209

Lower East Side trendsetters and Wall Street power players alike have been frequenting Freeman's since it opened in 2006. Originally located inside the men's clothing boutique but since spread into its own shop and other outposts in the city, Freemans offers not just top-notch haircuts and shaves ($42 each or $78 for the combo), but also services like the Hangover Treatment ($25), which includes a foaming gel mask, aromatic hot towels and a stress-relieving facial massage. It's walk-in only here, but the wait is usually minimal, just enough time to appreciate the charm of the vintage interior filled with displays of antique brushes and straight razors.

Rudy's Barbershop

14 W 29th, New York, NY 10001
(212) 532-7200

Before hitting NYC, Rudy's Barbershop was a hit in Seattle, where it first opened its doors in 1993, before expanding to LA and Portland. With a reputation to uphold and a mark to make on the city, Rudy's chose to set up shop just next door to the trendy Ace Hotel. The space, co-designed by Brooklyn's WRK Design, has a casual old-fashioned vibe to it, complete with antique doors and window frames made from salvaged hunting-rifle parts. Buzz cuts start at $17, with standard cuts running $40 for men and $60 for women. Lucky Ace Hotel guests cop can count on a 10% discount on cuts and 15% off the products found on the second floor retail area.

Tomcats Barbershop

135 India Street, Brooklyn, NY 11222
(718) 349-9666

Tomcats is kitschy central, with an impressive array of knickknacks for you to observe while you listen to some music and down a complimentary PBR. Traditional straight razor shaves run $30 while clipper cuts are only $20, and since the couple that owns the joint previously ran a motorcycle shop, you can still bring in your helmet for Tomcats' on-site pin striping and artwork service for $65/hr. Now that's definitely not something you can do at Supercuts!

TATTOOS

Getting a tattoo is special. Unlike most things in life, a tattoo is truly yours and yours alone. Of all the mediums through which artists express themselves, tattoo art may be the most personal, and since New York is home to some of the best artists in the world, making the major life decision of getting a tattoo is instantly easier. If a tattoo is in your future, it's important to choose a shop that is safe and clean and an artist that is responsive to your questions. If they are legendary for having created some one of a kind pieces for celebrities then that's cool too. If you're in New York and want to get stamped by the best, these are some shops that are known for their creativity and artistic flair.

Bang Bang NYC

328 Broome Street, New York, NY 10002
(212) 219-2799

Most likely, you've probably heard of Keith McCurdy, known as Bang Bang (thanks to his double pistol neck art) before, as he's the artist that's responsible for tattooing the most expensive, temperamental canvases imaginable: celebrity skin. After leaving East Side Ink, Bang Bang opened his own shop on Clinton Street and then in late 2014 moved to a new space on Broome, where with a roster of top-notch artists he knows and trusts, he's been tattooing the likes of Justin Bieber, Rihanna and Miley Cyrus. But you don't have to be famous to get a tattoo from this crew: with prices starting at $300, sure it's a bit steep, but anyone can get one.

East Side Ink

97 Avenue B, New York, NY 10009
(212) 477-2060

For nearly 20 years, neighborhood locals have been getting tattoos at East Side Ink, a popular shop with a staff of over ten artists, many of whom have won awards for their work. As a result, a wide variety of tattoo styles are represented: bold colors, black and grey, old school, new school, Japanese sleeves, pop art and more. And for the ladies that might get a little shy about getting a thigh piece done by a man, you'll be pleased to know that there are more women on staff here than at most tattoo studios. There is a $100 minimum and $200 an hour for larger pieces is standard.

Inkstop Tattoo

209 Avenue A, New York, NY 10009
(212) 995-2827

Eric Rignall opened Inkstop shortly after the ban on tattoo parlors was lifted back in 1997 and has been tattooing enthusiasts from all walks of life since then. The artists at Inkstop, all native New Yorkers, have a variety of styles covered: some like Eric himself specialize in fine lines and realistic pieces while others like Jose Soto concentrate on Japanese styles and religious iconography. Inkstop is open until 9pm on weekdays and 11pm on weekends.

NY Adorned

47 2nd Avenue, New York, NY 10003
(212) 473-0007

The recently renovated New York Adorned tattoo shop boasts an impressive array of resident artists (Adorned recently closed its Brooklyn location, so all of its talented artists and piercers are now under one roof at the 2nd Avenue location) and a constant rotation of guest artists. Every style of tattooing is represented at the shop, from eye-popping Japanese back pieces by renowned tattoo artist Horizakura to classic Americana in modern colors by Kris Magnotti.
Rates here range from $100 to $200 for the hour, which should be considered a bargain for getting tattooed at one of the most famous shops in the city.

Sacred Tattoo

424 Broadway #2, New York, NY 10013
(212) 226-4286

Nestled in between bustling Chinatown and trendy Soho, Sacred Tattoo's location perfectly reflects the duality found within this tattoo institution. Sacred is not your typical tattoo parlor: straddling the art world and tattoo culture, Sacred's 3,000 square foot space includes an art gallery featuring paintings and sculpture evocative of both current trends and sub-culture art. There are nearly twenty resident artists here all with varying styles, working daily from noon to 8pm.

Three Kings

572 Manhattan Avenue, Brooklyn, NY 11222
(718) 349-7755

There are over a dozen resident tattoo artists and a half dozen guest artists working at Three Kings seven days a week, so even though some artists may be booked an entire year in advance, walk-ins are always welcome. If you can't find someone who can do the design you want here, chances are that person doesn't exist. Three Kings takes a lot of pride in the consulting aspect of tattooing, talking you through the process from design to maintenance, a good way to ensure you don't end up getting a tattoo of your ex-girlfriend's name on your lower back or something. Prices here are pretty standard and they tattoo from noon to 10pm.

East Side Ink

GIRLS' NIGHT OUT

"Girls Night Out" is really something no man can ever understand. They spend extraordinary amounts of time planning, from the location of the event and the outfits they will wear to what they will order and drink throughout the night. The most important step in the process however, and often the most difficult, is selecting the right restaurant. In order to engage in a proper night of debauchery, a proper GNO needs to start off with a trendy, bustling restaurant to set the tone for an epic night to come. It's crucial for the backdrop to look as good as the women, so these are some of the trendiest and most female-friendly places to plan your next GNO.

L'Artusi

228 West 10th Street, New York, NY 10014
(212) 255-5757

L'Artusi is a West Village hotspot that offers a contemporary twist on traditional Italian favorites. The main room is set up perfectly as a succession of white marble bars. Your first stop will be the booze bar, obviously, where you'll get your hands on a glass of wine before moving toward the next slab, this time digging in to some aged parmesan at the cheese bar.
Then you'll settle in the sky-lit upstairs dining room and go to town on Chef Gabe Thompson's rustic pasta dishes: he serves things like potato gnocchi with a simple tomato sauce, fettuccine with rabbit cacciatore, and pici with peekytoe crab. The vibe here is upbeat, from hit music playing in the background to the dim lighting and modern decor.

Beauty & Essex

146 Essex Street, New York, NY 10002
(212) 614-0146

Beauty & Essex was practically created for the sole purpose of a girl's night out. You'll enter through an operational pawnshop, go through a disguised door in the back and suddenly find yourself inside a swanky bi-level restaurant with a 60's chic vibe. Chef Chris Santos has accessorized his signature shared plates with bountiful raw bar offerings, creative twists on *bruschetta* cleverly named "Jewels on Toast," and a selection of prime meats anchored by the show-stopping Dry Aged Bone-in Ribeye and feta-topped Beauty & Essex Lamb Burger. Even the ladies room serves complimentary champagne.

Tao Downtown

92 9th Avenue, New York, NY 10011
(212) 888-2724

From the restaurant's majestic decor with an ancient Asian feel to the world-renowned food, there's nothing not to love about this place. Tao Downtown takes up multiple spaces, with a restaurant, bar and lounge, a large main dining area, and a separate lounge. The menu here is perfect for sharing and draws inspiration from all over Asia, featuring dishes like a Hong Kong-style crispy snapper, Shanghainese fried rice stuffed in an egg crepe, and Japanese *wagyu sukiyaki*. The two focal points of the restaurant are the huge Buddha statue, and the wide, long, grand staircase leading from the bar area down to the main dining room. The combination of the two really creates a dramatic, dark and sexy vibe. The music is always fun and the noise is never unbearable, so you can still have a conversation and chair dance at the same time.

Yerba Buena Perry

1 Perry Street, New York, NY 10014
(212) 620-0808

Yerba Buena Perry is a combination of everything that's right about Latin American food. The Mexican chef's dishes combine a wide range of Caribbean and South American flavors in dishes like pork belly arepas, chorizo, fish tacos, ceviches, short ribs and a new

addition, dry aged steaks served with four different dipping sauces. The "Trio Of Fries" is a must have, because instead of potatoes, you get avocado, hearts of palm and watermelon. The decor of this West Village gem is reminiscent of an old-school Cuban dining club, with tropical wallpaper and paintings of a bygone Havana, black and white tiled floors and a massive mahogany bar. Delicious cocktails like the "Sun-dia", excellent service and a prime downtown location make this another go-to spot for a GNO.

Catch

21 9th Avenue, New York, NY 10014
(212) 392-5978

It is no understatement to say that Catch is the most over-the-top, ridiculous dining operation the Meatpacking District has ever seen. Inside the two floor, 14,000sf, 260 seat space, you'll run into models, suits, your typical older guys with young female companions and large groups of ladies enjoying a GNO. In Meatpacking District fashion, the menu starts off with a $100 Oysters & Bubbles option. Then come large-format plates like oversized Cantonese-style lobster, a crispy whole snapper with chili and garlic that's big enough to feed six, weighty whole branzino, and, of course, towers of raw shellfish. A glass-enclosed rooftop lounge offering panoramic views and cocktails for about two hundred pretty people keeps the party going.

Catch

THE MET'S ROOFTOP

Much like the first time someone goes to Paris they have an obligation to visit the Louvre, no first timer in New York should avoid a trip to the Metropolitan Museum of Art. However, like all of the world's best museums, the hordes of tourists make it an unappealing attraction to the locals, so we bypass the crowded exhibition halls and head straight for the elevator behind the lobby and up to the fifth floor's Roof Garden.

During the warm months, visitors can sip specialty martinis themed for the exhibitions at the museum while taking in spectacular unobstructed views of Central Park, the West Side and Midtown's skyline. There is always a special exhibit on the roof: in 2012, "Cloud City" by Tomas Saraceno, a magnificent, perception-changing installation was on display and in 2014, American artist Dan Graham designed "Hedge Two-Way Mirror Walkabout," a transparent and reflective structure that was part garden maze, part modernist skyscraper façade and created a changing and visually complex environment for visitors.

The bulk of the guests in the evenings are young New York professionals in their twenties and thirties having a few cocktails and perhaps listening to some music before heading out for the night, but no matter who you are or where you come from, being on top of the Met and looking out at the park below you and the city around you is something everyone will enjoy.

Roof Garden Café & Martini Bar

(open may to october)
Metropolitan Museum of Art
1000 5th Avenue #5, New York, NY 10028
(212) 535-7710

The Met's Rooftop

CIGARS

New York suffered the smoking ban that went into effect in March of 2003 without much of a fight. Since then it's been illegal to open new cigar bars, but there's a loophole: those that already existed before the ban are allowed to remain open, and new cigar stores are still allowed to open. So although the city's steak houses and social clubs have been forced to turn their humidors into storage space, there are still plenty of places to enjoy a cocktail and a cigar, even if it means bringing your own booze to the party.

The Cigar Inn

1016 2nd Avenue, New York, NY 10022
(212) 750-0809

The Cigar Inn is one of these places that doesn't sell alcohol, but members are allowed to store their own in a private locker. Not only can you buy premium cigars and sip on a glass of wine you've brought in yourself, but you can also peruse the store and gaze at their selection of cufflinks, money clips, and pens. The decor is a true homage to the historically clubby spaces and private libraries of Manhattan where cigar smoking was once prevalent. Come alone or with friends and bypass the barber chairs in the front, follow the long Persian runner that leads you away from Second Avenue, past the accessories, and select a fine cigar to smoke as you lounge in one of the comfortable leather armchairs.

Club Macanudo

26 East 63rd Street, New York, NY 10065
(212) 752-8200

What about of the lost practice of dining and smoking? Club Macanudo, the opulent club owned by General Cigar Co., one of the world's largest makers of handmade cigars, comprises a large, cavernous series of pilastered rooms, sculpted ceilings and leather couches, all bathed in subdued lighting. In the back of the club, opposite the wall of humidified cigar lockers, is the restaurant, where you'll want to reserve a table to enjoy steaks, lamb and veal chops or fish. Club Macanudo has managed to preserve the city's age-old practice of smoking a cigar before, during and after your meal, something you can't even do in Las Vegas anymore. The cigar menu is quite extensive, offering a large portfolio of General's cigars, as well as a few third-party brands.

Lexington Bar & Books

1020 Lexington Avenue, New York, NY 10021
(212) 717-3902

With three bar locations across Manhattan, the Bar & Books group offers a cigar and cocktail for every taste, but the Lexington Avenue location is where you want to be. This location attracts a professional, mature crowd and has a dress code that the tuxedo clad Maitre D that welcomes you will enforce. The bar has an extensive Scotch list, innovative cocktails, book-lined walls (though the lighting inside is very dim, so most will limit their reading what's on the menu), a fireplace in the back and always a James Bond movie playing on the single television screen. The kitchen serves up small plates and pizzas, the wine list is well rounded, and the cigar menu is solid.

Diamante's Brooklyn Cigar Lounge

108 South Oxford Street, Brooklyn, NY 11217
(646) 462-3876

Located within one of the cities classic historic brownstone buildings in the Fort Greene section of Brooklyn, Diamante's is one of the best places to enjoy a nice cigar in New York. The inside looks to be about a century-and-a-half old, with its unvarnished wooden flooring and copper ceiling, leather furniture, old fixtures and ancient photos of owner David Diamante's family, but the place has actually only been around since 2009. Open every day of the week, Diamante's is the perfect place to have a smoke while being entertained by a variety of events, including like live jazz. The glass humidor above the bar is packed with name brands like Padrón, Tatuaje, Dominican versions of Cohiba, Montecristo and Romeo y Julieta, and Diamante's own brand of hand rolled cigars separated into mild-, medium- and full-bodied. A ridiculously low corkage fee is an incentive to bring your own selection of booze to accompany your cigar.

OTHER OPTIONS

Merchants NY Cigar Bar

1125 1ˢᵗ Avenue, Manhattan, NY 10065
(212) 832-4610

Velvet Cigar Lounge

13 East 7ᵗʰ Street, New York, NY 10003
(212) 533-5582

The Cigar Inn

DENIM

The perfect pair of jeans is like the white whale of clothing, a must have in every New Yorker's wardrobe and yet extremely elusive if you don't commit to finding it. When it comes to purchasing top-notch raw denim in New York, there's certainly no shortage of stores that can cater to your needs. Nowhere is the "premium denim" craze more prevalent than in the boutiques of New York's Nolita and Soho, which are chock full of high-fashion finds to fit any budget, but each store has its own specialties to meet your denim needs, so be sure to not limit yourself to just one.

Atrium

644 Broadway, New York, NY 10012
(212) 473-9200

This perennial favorite for denim oddly resembles an old-fashioned train station, from the wrought iron transom above the wide entryway to the white marble floor and gold girders crisscrossing the high ceiling. If you're looking for a serene shopping experience, you might want to bring your earplugs since there's frequently an in-house DJ spinning hip-hop while customers browse rack after rack of denim labels like Joe's, Nudie, Prps, AG Jeans and J Brand, along with shoes and accessories for men and women.

Jean Shop

435 West 14ᵗʰ Street, New York, NY 10014
(212) 366-5326

A denim destination since 2003, the Jean Shop, named one of the top 100 stores in the USA by GQ magazine, specializes in handcrafted washes and distress patterns, all designed on a case-by-case basis for style-savvy customers. If you're looking for a unique pair, these guys can whip you up a custom wash on top of top-notch Japanese selvage. Those in a rush can skip the five-day-long wait for made-to-measure pants and snap up premade styles that are just as well-crafted, while those in the market for something other than jeans can peruse the selection of leather jackets, belts and wallets that also bear the signature styled-in-house look.

Blue In Green

8 Greene Street, New York, NY 10013
(212) 680-0555

Blue In Green is widely regarded as one of the top places to buy raw denim in the world. You'll buzz in order to enter this men's lifestyle boutique where they carry an impressive selection of cult and rare Japanese denim, including brands such as Japan Blue, Eternal, Left Field, Momotaro and Samurai. Prices range from the low three figures all the way up to four figures for a pair by Kyuten, embedded with ground pearl and strips of rare vintage kimono. An assortment of street clothes and limited-edition shoes from brands like Stone Island, Low Hurtz, and Paul Smith provide the rest of what you need for your casual cool look.

Self Edge

157 Orchard Street, New York, NY 10002
(212) 388-0079

Self Edge predominantly stocks denim from sought-after Japanese brands including The Flat Head, Iron Heart and Sugar Cane & Co., as well as American brands Roy and 3sixteen. The main value that Self Edge offers is that they specialize in reproductions of vintage Americana denim from the 20s-50s à la Japanese denim and designers. Almost uniformly, they're broodingly dark and ramrod stiff, recreating rugged American denim products of decades long gone. This is not where you come to shop for summer clothes. They also provide a full range of denim services, including repairs and chain stitch hems.

Brooklyn Denim Company

85 N 3rd St #101, Brooklyn, NY 11249
(718) 782-2600

Located in Williamsburg, it is akin to a denim museum complete with the customer service you would expect from a Michelin starred restaurant. The store offers an expansive and unique selection of denim that can fit any style or budget, and the knowledgeable staff has what it takes to find just the right pair for the right customer. The selection of 20-plus brands includes small West-coast companies as well as locally made "one offs" exclusive to the store and not available online. In addition to the racks of jeans ranging, the store also stocks a selection of vintage workwear from Pendleton and Levi's and an in-house tailor will even hem your jeans pro bono.

3x1

15 Mercer Street, New York, NY 10013
(212) 391-6969

The experienced tailors at 3x1 can make you a pair of jeans that are perfectly custom-fitted to your body - quite literally the perfect pair of jeans for you made from denim material from multiple mills in Japan as well as Cone Mills in North Carolina. The bespoke service doesn't come cheap though, with prices starting around $1200. If that's beyond your price range, don't worry, they also offer a selection of jeans in regulated fits at the store that doubles as a factory.

(DENIM OUNCE WEIGHT CHART)
AN 60 DIFFERENT SELVEDGE DENIMS FROM MILLS AND SUPPLIERS LIKE:
CT, CONE, DENIM AREA, KURABO & KAIHARA (TO NAME JUST A FEW).

MID

HEAVY

NOVELTY

10   11   12   13   14   15   16   18

3x1

WATERFRONT BARS

Summer in New York can mean many things, but the one constant will always be the heat. Heat so intense that if a place doesn't have air conditioning, you can be sure no one's setting foot inside. But even the best air conditioning in the world doesn't make up for letting a beautiful day go by without enjoying the outside. When a walk through the neighborhood is more skyscraper than palm tree, it's easy to forget that we live on an island, but just like the tropical islands of our dream vacations, New York is filled with waterfront bars and restaurants to cool down at with a cold drink and a magnificent view.

Pier-i Cafe

500 West 70th Street, New York, NY 10023
(212) 362-4450

The Pier i Café, set on the esplanade along the Hudson River around 68th Street, is an outdoor bar and grill with two dozen shaded tables and comfortable lounge chairs. Beer, sangria and wine cool you down as you watch the sun set over the river and pick at burgers and fries, and nothing, considering you are by the water, is priced too expensive. Acoustic musicians lend a tropical vibe, there's salsa on Sunday nights, and the café also provides a prime vantage point for Summer on the Hudson: Movies Under the Stars, a series of free screenings every Wednesday at 8:30pm put on by the Parks Department.

Frying Pan

530 West 26th Street, New York, NY 10001
(212) 989-6363

The Frying Pan, a 1929 lightship that spent three years at the bottom of the Chesapeake before it was salvaged and converted into a bar, has become one of the city's biggest summertime hot spots. Seating is first come, first served and it crowds up fast with people wanting to enjoy buckets of 6 Coronas from the tiki bar or burgers from the grill, so arrive early to grab a seat and enjoy the breeze. Fridays, Turntables on the Hudson, one of the city's oldest outdoor dance parties, holds court inside the boat's sinister hull or on the pier, but if you've had a couple or are easily seasick, perhaps staying on land might be wiser than trying to sync your rhythm with the undulating dance floor.

Pier-i Cafe

Crow's Nest

The East River between 28th & 32nd Street,
New York, NY 10016
(212) 683-3333

The Crow's Nest can be found on the upper deck of a yacht permanently docked on the East River around 30th Street. More of a piano bar than an outdoor party, you come here for a more relaxed atmosphere, to sip a few refined cocktails and enjoy the seafood shack bar menu while taking in the sweeping views of Manhattan, Brooklyn, Queens and the East River. And if it rains, and you have a few bucks to spare, the nautical-themed restaurant downstairs will ensure you don't get soaked.

Boat Basin Café

West 79th Street, New York, NY 10024
(212) 496-5542

One of the city's most picturesque and popular outdoor gathering spots is the 79th Street Boat Basin. On a clear night, with the sun setting interminably over the Palisades across the river, an eclectic mix of New Yorkers, ranging from high heeled partiers starting their night on the town to shorts and flip flop wearing groups coming from the park, sip on strong margaritas and beers on the spacious patio. With the boats bobbing in the water directly in front, the Boat Basin feels like an exclusive yacht club, except everyone is invited to this party.

Ruby's Bar & Grill

1213 Boardwalk West, Brooklyn, NY 11224
(718) 975-7829

Ruby's is the epitome of the beach bar even though it started off in 1928 as a cabaret. Salty ocean air wafts through the bar's open façade, beer is sipped out of plastic cups, mismatched furniture provides seating and a great jukebox belts out Sinatra and Perry Como hits. Old Coney Island photographs plaster the walls and guys that may have been children in those black and white photos now line the lengthy bar, giving the place the look and feel of a true timeless classic. Leave them the bar and grab a seat overlooking the boardwalk for some interesting people watching.

Pier A Harbor House

22 Battery Place, New York, NY 10004
(212) 785-0153

With Ulysses and The Dead Rabbit already under his belt, Peter Poulakakos is a veteran entrepreneur in the Financial District, so when a pier closed to the public for 127 years was up for grabs, he went in to do his thing. The historic landmark is now Pier A, a three-story construction featuring 6 venues, each offering breathtaking views of New York Harbor and its centerpiece, the Statue of Liberty. The first floor includes a bar incredibly featuring dark & stormys and Pimm's cups on tap, an oyster bar and an expansive beer hall. The more intimate second floor houses a cocktail bar as well as an upscale steakhouse-like restaurant paying homage to the Hudson Valley. The third floor is reserved for special events, but with the first two to play in, nobody's going to feel cheated.

FOOD TRUCKS

The city that never sleeps loves to eat, and for the New Yorker on the move, the concept of mobile eateries is a match made in heaven. While the phenomenon of food trucks has caught on in several cities throughout the country, there is an unparalleled diversity of offerings here that is representative of the cultural melting pot that is New York City. Anywhere you go, you can see food trucks whipping up a variety of cuisines, from Mexican and Greek to Indian and French, including plenty of cross over fusions. It's hard to know where to begin, but with Twitter, facebook and a myriad of websites keeping you connected to your favorites, at least you'll never have to worry about making reservations again.

Comme Ci, Comme Ça

@Chefsamirtruck

Chef Samir was born and raised in Casablanca, and when he came to New York, he quickly found joy in cooking his mother's recipes for his friends in the city, soon he was introducing all New Yorkers to *tajines* and *couscous*. A master griller, he uses a flame grill instead of a flat top in order to give each piece of meat a delicious char grilled flavor. His *Couscous Royale* includes frilled beef, chicken, grilled lamb and *merguez* – a carnivore's paradise! The truck moves around often, so it's imperative to check where he is going to be from one day to the next, and whether you decide on a couscous, a *kofta* brochette or some *tilapia* over Basmati rice, make sure to taste the four special sauces that all add layers of flavor to Chef Samir's affordable gourmet meals.

Snowday

@SnowdayTruck

The Snowday food truck is known for various things depending on who you ask. For some, it's a destination for maple-syrup themed foods using ingredients strictly sourced from local farms. Others see Snowday as a truck owned and operated by Drive Change, a New York-based non-profit organization that focuses on providing training and steady employment for formerly incarcerated youth in hopes of helping them find work and keeping them out of prison. Combined, it's a recipe that attracts the hungry masses who want to support the cause while eating delicious things like the maple cheddar grilled sandwich, maple curry chicken salad or maple bacon fried Brussels sprouts. Snowday operates year round but is always on the move so make sure to track their daily movements.

Desi Truck

@DesiFoodTruck

The Desi Truck is always parked on the corner of 6th Ave near Spring St. A former Vendy Award finalist (the Oscars for Food Trucks), the Desi Truck has earned quite a loyal and respected following by serving classics such as chicken *tikka masala* over rice and salad and flaky kati rolls stuffed with chicken, *paneer masala*, or *aloo masala*, Almageer, the owner who opened this truck in 2010 because of a perceived "lack of tasty Indian street foods in my beloved city," also serves *haleem*, a dense stew made of meat, lentils and wheat made into a thick paste. It's a time consuming dish to prepare, six hours at least for the stew to reach the tight consistency, and on a cold winter day, the distinctly Indian flavors of this dish will warm you to the core.

Korilla BBQ

@KorillaBBQ

This Korean-inspired taco truck can usually be found in office-heavy midtown Manhattan every day of the week. Korilla BBQ is famous for their various kimchis and sauces that you can pile on to your choice of proteins, such as "Ribeye of the Tiger" (bulgogi made from black angus ribeye steaks) or "Wonder Bird" (marinated chicken thigh). Vegetarians can opt for the thick slices of homemade tofu, but no matter which way you go, it's a lot of fun getting messy with all the toppings.

Morris Truck

@morristruck

The grilled cheese craze has taken over New York to the point where we now have so many grilled cheese trucks now roaming the streets, it can be hard to pick one to highlight. The Morris Truck stands out by keeping it simple. At times it offers options like gouda with pork jowl or pastrami with chimichurri, but the classic grilled cheese, with NY State Cheddar and New Hampshire Landaff cheeses griddled between two slices of thin, perfectly browned bread, is as close to the ultimate traditional comfort food as you're going to get.

El Diablo Tacos

@ElDiabloTacos

If only every bar in New York could follow Union Pool's lead the city would be better for it: in the back patio, the Williamsburg hotspot has a parked taco truck serving *tamales, tortas*, roasted corn and tacos (chicken, pork, beef, vegetarian, fish and shrimp) from 7pm until 3:30am. When Union Pool fires up its backyard bonfire in the winter, taco truck is the perfect way to make sure the whiskey and beer have something nice to play with in your stomach.

The Halal Guys

Not a truck, but not to be missed, 53ʳᵈ & 6ᵗʰ

Their famous carts are located on 53ʳᵈ and 6ᵗʰ Avenue, all day and night. They serve chicken and lamb on rice, the quintessential New York "street meat" platter, and there's a reason people are willing to drive in from New Jersey for a taste. Perfectly spiced and tender chunks of meat are layered on top of yellow or white rice and doused in their signature white and hot sauce. But beware of imposters! Other carts have set up shop on the same block serving similar food while their employees wear nearly identical uniforms, so keep an eye out.

CHINATOWN

Manhattan's Chinatown is a thriving representation of the American Dream in action, home to one of the densest populations of Chinese immigrants in the western hemisphere. The thriving immigrant population in Chinatown gives visitors access to strange culinary delights and to the sense of tradition it has preserved amidst the ever-changing landscape of the city. Chinatown can be one of the most fun neighborhoods in New York if you know where to go, and especially where to avoid.

Nom Wah Tea Parlor

13 Doyers Street, New York, NY 10013
(212) 962-6047

Originally opened in 1920, it retains the old-timey charm that has kept it popular. Long time regulars and newcomers alike rave over the roast pork bun, a fluffy and moist bun filled with sizeable chunks of quality meat and caramelized onions. Unlike most *dim sum* houses, at Nom Wah you order off of a menu, ensuring fresh food made to order. Traditional Chinese shrimp dumplings, egg rolls and pan-fried noodle dishes are also to be enjoyed in the strange Art Deco style dining room.

Golden Unicorn

18 East Broadway, New York, NY 10002
(212) 941-0911

The antithesis of Nom Wah, a sprawling multi-level restaurant in an office building with ballroom banquet halls and dragons with glowing eyes covering the walls. Seven days a week, fresh *dumplings*, platters of chicken feet and even shark fin soup are paraded through the crowds on carts. Unless you come as a big group, you'll find yourself sharing a table with local Chinese residents, allowing for one of my favorite food related games - I'll have what they're having. No matter what you try, you'll find the Cantonese offerings here delightfully subtle, expertly prepared and seasoned. After all, if you take a look at the crowd around you, these are people who know what to expect from good *dim sum*.

Tasty Dumpling

54 Mulberry Street, New York, NY 10013
(212) 349-0070

Many places in Chinatown offer 4 or 5 *dumplings* for around a buck, but at Tasty Dumpling, they are filled with marinated meat that makes the filling juicier and tastier than anywhere else. On top of that, Tasty Dumplings' new and bigger location is more inviting than a lot of *dumpling* shops.

Golden Unicorn

Big Wing Wong

102 Mott Street, New York, NY 10013
(212) 274-0696

Roasted duck is the kind of signature dish that defines a whole cuisine. Big Wing Wong, also known as 102 Noodles Town (because that's what the sign outside inexplicably says), has the best in the neighborhood. As soon as you bite into a slice, with its fatty, succulent meat and crackling, burnished mahogany skin, you won't care if the restaurant has ten names. Let the bird speak for itself and don't drown it in side sauces like *hoisin*: accompany the duck with a bowl of *wonton* noodles covered with pork and shrimp.

Bread Talk

47 Catherine Street, New York, NY 10038
(917) 832-4784

Dan-Tat is a Hong-Kong style egg tart that is the perfect end to any meal in Chinatown, but don't go grabbing the first one you come across. Bread Talk is a bit on the outskirts of Chinatown, away from the hustle and bustle, but worth the walk because every bite into the buttery, crispy and flaky crust that holds the sweet egg-flavored filling will entice you to order another dozen to take home with you. And at 2 for $1, you may end up doing just that.

Yunhong Chopsticks

50 Mott Street, New York, NY 10013
(212) 566-8828

As everyone who orders Chinese takeout in New York knows, restaurants are becoming increasingly stingy with their chopsticks, so when you're in Chinatown, Yunhong Chopsticks is a must, at least once. You can pick up a pretty plastic set to keep in the kitchen drawer for a few bucks, or go all out with an ebony mahogany set with German silver tips for $600, a perfect gift for the person who already has everything. As the wallpaper on the shop's back wall explains, the Chinese tradition of giving chopsticks spreads happiness, so don't pass up the unique experience of chopstick shopping in Chinatown.

Posteritati

239 Centre Street, New York, NY 10013
(212) 226-2207

Posteritati is well known as maybe the very best store around for cinema posters. With more than 12,000 posters available in the store and access to countless more through their impressive database, this is an excellent place to search for a gift for a film fanatic. Posterati is also just fun to visit because it functions as a gallery space as well, displaying mini-exhibits that rotate several times a year.

Downtown Music Gallery

13 Monroe Street, New York, NY 10002
(212) 473-0043

A basement in Chinatown filled with over 6,000 CDs and vinyl LPs (the rest are off-site and can be ordered online) that make up the city's most impressive selection of avant-garde jazz, contemporary and progressive rock. For a place so immersed in the music scene, it is refreshing to find an unpretentious staff eager to help you discover new music. Occasionally they even have live shows playing, ideal to discover tunes you might want to take home.

ROOFTOPS

For the city's trendiest hotels, no amenity is as sweet or as touted as a pool, a bar, or a restaurant on high, and since this is New York we're talking about, all of these venues have mindboggling views. Going alfresco can be a liberating experience: most obviously, there's fresh air, but more subtly there's this sense as a New Yorker that after a day spent trying to crawl your way to the top, you've finally made it in a way. Stylish, hip, modern or classic, whether you're looking for an epic party or chill vibes with a foodie menu, we've got you covered.

Gallow Green

542 West 27th Street, New York, NY 10001
(212) 564-1662

The rooftop of the McKittrick Hotel, home of the interactive play Sleep No More, is an enchanting garden filled with dark dens and even an entire vine covered antique train car, a relaxing place to process what you've just witnessed. A floor of pebbles and slate, trellises woven with flowers and weathered wooden tables recall an upstate country home left adorably to seed. But as the sun descends over the Hudson and the gleaming West Side buildings, and as darkness encroaches, Christmas lights encircling small trees and the rafters overhead blink to life while a brass band waltzes dizzyingly through tunes. Nothing is done halfway here: there's just an obscene attention to detail that will either make you wonder how quickly you can see the show again, or, if you just came for drinks, how soon you can get tickets for it.

Plunge Rooftop Bar & Lounge

18 9th Avenue, New York, NY 10014
(212) 660-6736

It's impossible to think of rooftop bars in New York without mentioning the longstanding best, Plunge at the Gansevoort Hotel. It's hard to believe that the flagship party-hard hotel is more than a decade old, but the rooftop pool and vibrant bar haven't lost their luster. The elevator will take you to the 15th floor where you exit directly into the bar area, which is covered by a glass greenhouse-like structure when it's rainy or chilly. The pool is reserved for hotel guests and private events, but the lounge is where everything happens. If it's too crowded, the wraparound outdoor space is a great alternative to soak up the panorama of the Hudson River and New Jersey. Packed year round Plunge is best reserved for a Monday or Tuesday night to have a cocktail and gaze at Midtown's skyscrapers in peace.

Press Lounge

653 11ᵗʰ Avenue, New York, NY 10036
(212) 757-2224

The Press Lounge, on the 16ᵗʰ floor of the Ink 48 Hotel in Hell's Kitchen boasts spectacular views of the New York skyline as well as a captivating glowing 70-foot-long reflecting pool and a glass enclosed lounge. It draws a mixed but generally young crowd, and feels much less stuffy than comparable hotel bars on the east side. The drink prices here are reasonable and the light fare surprisingly delicious (the goat cheese gnocci is a must). Because of its location so far west, you'll miss some of New York's best known buildings, but the unobstructed view of the sun setting over the Hudson River is why the midtown crowd congregates here after work.

Salon De Ning

700 5ᵗʰ Avenue, New York, NY 10019
(212) 956-2888

Everything here is built to resemble the salon of a jet-setting, eccentric, 1930's Shanghai socialite named Madame Ning. The chic and sophisticated East meets West décor attracts a more polished clientele than other rooftops: during the day, Upper East Side ladies stop by after a Bergdorf Goodman shopping excursion; at dusk, local financiers have a drink after work. The velvet ropes have been traded in for private terraces tricked out with luxurious oriental daybeds and stellar views of Fifth Avenue, Manhattan's

skyline, and the Hudson River, while inside, glowing lanterns illuminate tiny tables. Grab a couple *Ning Slings* and settle in for a sunset cocktail experience that's guaranteed to seal any deal you're looking to close.

Upstairs

145 East 50ᵗʰ Street, New York, NY 10022
(212) 702-1600

Upstairs offers 360-degree views of the city. Three separate indoor/outdoor atmospheres complete the 3,000 square foot venue making it possible to enjoy a bird's eye view of the iconic Chrysler Building in both winter and summer. The bar is a stunning mixture of punk rock and the Louvre. Great variety of cocktails by world renowned mixologists, as well as an international wine list and a fine selection of beers.

The Ides

80 Wythe Avenue, New York, NY 11211
(718) 460-8004

Williamsburg's hippest rooftop drinking destination, located on the 6ᵗʰ floor of the Wythe Hotel. The indoor and outdoor bar offers a seasonal drink menu, a large terrace, and a breathtaking view of the Manhattan skyline. No food is served up at the bar so grab a bite downstairs and then head up for a cocktail, settle into one of the red banquettes and let the panorama sink in.

Plunge Rooftop Bar & Lounge

The Ides

BURGERS

Like most American foods, the burger has immigrant origins, but it is American innovation that has made it the feel good sandwich that we know and love today. In New York, where some of the greatest culinary minds fight each day to stand out, the burger has morphed into a creation that sometimes barely resembles it's origins as a beef patty between two slices of white bread. In becoming so diverse, the New York burger landscape has made it impossibly hard to judge what the best burger in the city is.

Burger Joint

119 West 56th Street, New York, NY 10019
(212) 245-5000

You normally wouldn't head to a hotel for a great burger, but at the upscale Le Parker Meridien hotel, just past the reception, you'll see a neon sign in the shape of a hamburger indicating that there is something going on behind the floor to ceiling curtains. Push them apart and you enter a little coffee shop style tiny restaurant with faux-wood paneling, beaten up wooden tables, and a few sports-page photos taped to the graffiti-strewn walls. The menu is short: burgers, fries, drinks and milkshakes. Unlike in many places, the burger actually comes off a grill, adding a distinct flavor to the perfectly cooked meat, and the cheese, a mixture of White American and Colby cheeses, melts perfectly on top.

Minetta Tavern

113 Macdougal Street, New York, NY 10012
(212) 475-3850

With only 70 seats in two rooms, it has all the trademarks of a McNally restaurant: tiled floors, stained mirrors, vintage bar and red leather banquettes. It's a steakhouse in effect, but the specialty drawing in the crowds of models and movie honchos, along with those who want to be seen with them, is the Black Label Burger, a blend of 42-day dry aged rib-eye, short rib and brisket. It's served on a lightly toasted brioche bun from his Balthazar Bakery with caramelized onions and shoestring fries. The meat is bathed in clarified butter and doused in salt and pepper throughout the cooking process, and because of the aging process, it's tangy and pungent, a taste not found in your typical burger.

J.G. Melon

1291 3rd Avenue, New York, NY 10021
(212) 744-0585

Nothing satisfies a yearning for "old New York" better than a trip to JG Melon, that's been dishing out what I consider the city's best burgers since 1972. The burger itself is as simple, unpretentious and comforting as the atmosphere. The loosely packed patty is griddled to perfection, gently oozing juices through the charred crust to gently bathe the toasted bun it rests on and is served with red onions and pickles on the side to use at your discretion. A small bowl of cottage fries and a cold mug of beer is all you need to paint the picture of happiness.

Spotted Pig

314 West 11th Street, New York, NY 10014
(212) 620-0393

April Bloomfield is probably more responsible than anyone for the influx of high-end burgers in New York. Her West Village tavern, investors in which include Jay-Z and Bono, serves up a fantastic burger, big in size and flavor, with tangy crumbles of Roquefort on a pillowy brioche bun that is rather unconventionally toasted on both sides. It's served with shoestring fries but no lettuce or tomato, and don't even think of asking for a change to that order because they famously accept no requests for substitutions.

Fritzl's Lunch Box

173 Irving Avenue, New York, NY 11237
(929) 210-9531

Fritzl's is a perfect representation of the gentrification of the Bushwick neighborhood of Brooklyn. The décor is accented by red plastic chairs reminiscent of grade school, a high bookshelf lined with cookbooks, and a hanging hornet's nest in the window. Dan Ross-Leutwyler offers sophisticated takes on everyday food at affordable prices, and nowhere does it shine more than in the burger: a bold mixture of beef cheek and chuck cooked on a griddle, blanketed with two slices of sharp cheddar and placed on a toasted bun. The miso aioli and the finely chopped onion and pickle relish add a combination of flavors to this burger that alone is worth a trip to Bushwick.

Shake Shack

Multiple locations
East 23rd Street and Madison Avenue,
New York, NY 10010 (212) 889-6600

New York's answer to the legendary West Coast burger institution, on the scene in Madison Square Park since 2004 when Danny Meyer's cheeseburgers took the city by storm. The original in the park still reigns supreme, although the lines do too but the burger is worth the wait. With meat coming from Pat LaFrieda, like Minetta Tavern's, this high-end, a mix of brisket, chuck, and short rib, is cooked to order and served on a soft bun with gooey American cheese, lettuce and tomato. An order of the SmokeShack, a cheeseburger and a nice cold shake is the perfect way to enjoy a little break in the park while the city bustles around you.

SPAS

New York is exciting, but sometimes life in the Big Apple shifts into overdrive and becomes stressful. When chasing down and fighting for taxis and running around tourists who act like they've never walked on a sidewalk before has your stress and rage levels bubbling over, it's time to hit the pause button and relax. New York is filled with spas to lead you into a state of nirvana with the help of massages, body scrubs and other treatments that help you renew, refresh and rejuvenate.

As is true of everything in New York, some of these will cost you an arm and a leg, but others are affordable enough that the occasional massage won't mean you'll have to fall back on an all-ramen diet or anything.

Great Jones Spa

29 Great Jones Street, New York, NY 10012
(212) 505-3185

Great Jones Spa in downtown Manhattan is one of the loveliest spas in the city, known for its "wet lounge", available to guests for two hours prior to and one hour following spa treatments. These exceptional treatments are pricy but well worth it: the aromatherapy massage ($145 for 60 minutes) uses hot scented oils to promote relaxation, the river rock facial ($150 for 60 minutes) comes complete with a cold and heated stone wash followed by a repairing mask, and the Rosemary Citron Sea Salt Scrub ($150 for 60 minutes) involves a vigorous all-over scrub using Rosemary, Lemon Peel and Safflower Seed oil. The wet lounge has a 3-story waterfall, a thermal hot tub and cold plunge pool. A visit to the rock sauna is the perfect antidote to chilly city weather.

Aire Ancient Baths

88 Franklin Street, New York, NY 10013
(212) 274-3777

In ancient Greece and Rome, public bathhouses were large, extravagant places where people would lounge in various water pools to clean themselves and cure their ailments. New York City, for all its worldliness, has never had a world-class bathhouse, until now. Every bit of the sumptuous setting - the marble, the stone sinks, even the hundreds of candles that illuminate the subterranean space - was shipped over from Spain. The basement level of the gigantic three-story space houses the spacious, open room of baths, which consist of hot, cold, saltwater and multi-jet pools alongside steam and hot-stone rooms where you can lounge for up to two hours. Up the ante by adding a for extra relaxation. You can also book ultra-luxurious treatments, the Red Wine Ritual, the Olive Oil Ritual or the Kerala Ritual, which begin with a ritual soak, are followed by a massage, and end with a thermal bath experience. The types of soaks and massages differ by ritual, and the prices start around $500.

Ohm Spa

260 5th Avenue #7, New York, NY 10001
(212) 845-9812

Ohm Spa is not as luxurious as some of your other options, so don't expect elaborate facilities like hot tubs or steam showers, but the friendly staff here believes in custom-tailoring client treatments and performs the full gamut of services to perfection, from paraffin nail care to exfoliating facials to glorious massages. Most extravagant is the manicure room, where clients sit in iJoy massage chairs and watch movies on two flat-screen TVs. Popular treatments include the hot stone massage, the deep Swedish massage and their specialty Manuka honey facial. Instead of floral patterns, Ohm sports clean lines and a palette of sky blue and chocolate brown, gender-neutral hues that don't scare men away and attract the urban professionals who work nearby.

Body by Brooklyn

275 Park Avenue, Brooklyn, NY 11205
(718) 923-9400

Body By Brooklyn is one of New York's best-kept secrets, the creation of husband and wife team Mira and Alex Goldin who visited word renowned spas in France, Russia and Turkey while developing the concept for their spa. As a result, Body By Brooklyn feels like a decadent mix of all three cultures. Some packages let you

Body by Brooklyn

stay all day and spend an hour or two in the "Wet Lounge" which features a Russian and Swedish Sauna, a Turkish Aroma Steam Room, Soaking Pools and Jacuzzis. The Red Flower Hammam, wherein you're steamed, soaked, and beaten with oak leaves, will leave you supple and glowing for days. High-rollers book the Studio Suite, a stunning corner spot featuring a private Jacuzzi, steam room, couch, and plasma TV. Available for groups and events, the suite comes with hors d'oeuvres and a complimentary bottle of champagne. Night Spa, every other Monday night from 21h to 2h, invites people to take advantage of the spa while a DJ plays and drinks are served at the bar.

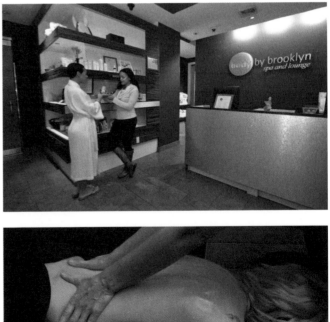

HIGH LINE

Few places in the city are more pleasant on a sunny afternoon. It used to be an elevated rail track that went out of use in 1980, and today the popular elevated green space has become a destination for sunbathing, sightseeing, snacking and viewing innovative art along the 1.45 mile long track that runs from the Meatpacking District to the northern edge of Chelsea. Filled with wildflowers and grasses, it offers a panorama of the bustle below. The charms of the park itself have been added to the streets below, which have blossomed since its opening. There are now nine sets of stairs to the park from street level, and new galleries, restaurants, boutiques, bars and even hotels keep popping up around them.

192 Books

192 10th Avenue, New York, NY 10011
(212) 255-4022

192 Books is a Chelsea book store, owned by art dealer Paula Cooper and her husband, editor Jack Macrae, that offers a strong selection of art books and literature, as well as memoirs and books on gardening, history, politics, design and music. Take a walk through the white-walled, high-ceilinged book emporium that resembles a private library and you're guaranteed to find something to flip through once you're settled on one of the High Line's wood-plank benches.

Standard Biergarten

848 Washington St, New York, NY 10014
(212) 645-4646

Typically teeming with a fashion-forward crowd, the Standard Hotel's beer garden directly underneath the High Line offers

communal seating for 200. The beers are purchased via a ticket system (tickets cost 8 bucks a pop). Ping-pong tables, pretzels as big as your head and a unique selection of beer, including Bitburger and Kostrizer & Licher, complement the full bar. If you're looking for a beer garden that's more of a see and be seen kind of drinking experience, this is where you should post up as soon as it gets nice out.

Blue Bottle Coffee

450 West 15th Street, New York, NY 10014
(510) 653-3394

Positioned right above the Chelsea Market near 14th Street, Blue Bottle's High Line outpost operates from April to November. The kiosk has a full espresso bar, single-origin drip coffee prepared to order and their amazing *New Orleans-styled* iced coffee (cold-brewed for 18 hours with roasted chicory), the perfect caffeine push to get you walking through

the park. They also serve delicious house-made pastries, and you can pick up a bag of beans to take home.

Chelsea Piers

23rd Street & Hudson River Park,
New York, NY 10011
(212) 336-6800

Chelsea Piers is a recreational complex that has been serving the needs of sporty New Yorkers for more than 15 years. If you're craving something more than a slow stroll through the park, make your way to the northern end of the High Line and stop by this waterfront sports village where golfers hit balls until midnight every day, while others take advantage of tennis courts, rock climbing walls, an indoor ice skating rink, batting cages and a bowling alley.

Milk Studios

450 West 15th Street, New York, NY 10011
(212) 645-2797

A beautiful and versatile studio space in Chelsea. The art gallery specializes in the works of photographers who document celebrity, fashion and pop-culture. The multi-level facility features high ceilings, large windows allowing plenty of sunlight, and a sleek, clean interior where you're as likely to see a show featuring work by Japanese Shinto sculpture Shinko Ito as you are a collection of never before seen photos of the Rat Pack.

Cookshop

156 10th Ave, New York, NY 10011
(212) 924-4440

The food at Cookshop is as American as it gets, the ingredients all sustainable and sourced from independent farmers. The market inspired menu changes frequently, and with an open kitchen featuring a wood-burning oven, rotisserie, and grill, everything from the roasted chicken with fire-charred fingerlings to the grilled Berkshire pork chop served with spiced sweet potato purée or the grilled Montauk squid with capers, lemon, and parsley hits the spot just right. With a bar facing the window and an outdoor space for when the weather is just right, you're just as likely to come to eat as to people watch.

Upright Citizens Brigade Theatre

307 West 26th Street, New York, NY 10001
(212) 366-9176

After a nice afternoon in the park, a visit to the Upright Citizens Brigade Theater is a perfect way to end the day. Improv shows at the UCB are a right of passage for many New York comedians and ASSSSCAT 3000, the long-running Sunday night show that regularly features guests whom you may recognize from Saturday Night Live and shows on Comedy Central, is definitely worth checking out.

AROUND THE WORLD

Everyone knows that New York is full of great food, which is a huge selling point, especially for those who live here and get to enjoy it 24/7. Despite what out-of-towners may think, our food is about more than just pizza and bagels: it's also about more than a century of immigrants who have imprinted their cultures into the way this city feeds and nurtures its residents. This is one of the most densely populated places in the world, and the backgrounds of the city's inhabitants are as diverse as you're likely to find anywhere.

While most foreign communities tend to stay close-knit, like the Asian community in Flushing, the Russians in Brighton Beach, the Greeks in Astoria or the Polish in Greenpoint, you don't need to travel to these enclaves to find traditional foreign foods. You could happily eat your way around the world without ever even leaving Manhattan!

These 25 restaurants represent the cuisines of their respective countries and present their traditional foods so authentically it almost feels like taking a vacation.

ARGENTINA ⓳

Buenos Aires
513 E 6th St, New York, NY 10009
(212) 228-2775

AUSTRALIA ⓴

Tuck Shop
68 E 1st St #1, New York, NY 10003
(212) 979-5200

AUSTRIA ㉓

Café Katja
79 Orchard St, New York, NY 10002
(212) 219-9545

BELGIUM ⑤

BXL East
210 E 51st Street, New York, NY 10022
(212) 888-7782

CUBA

Cuba
222 Thompson Street, New York, NY 10012
(212) 420-7878

CZECH REPUBLIC ❸

Café Prague
2 W 19th St, New York, NY 10011
(212) 929-2602

EGYPT ⓫

Casa La Femme
140 Charles Street, New York, NY 10014
(212) 505-0005

ETHIOPIA ❻

Queen of Sheba
650 10th Avenue, New York, NY 10036
(212) 397-0610

GERMANY ❷

Heidelberg
1648 2nd Avenue, New York, NY 10028
(212) 628-2332

JAMAICA ⓬

Miss Lily's
132 West Houston Street, New York, NY 10012
(646) 588-5375

INDIA ⓲

Brick Lane Curry House
306 E 6th Street, New York, NY 10003
(212) 979-2900

ISRAEL ❿

Taim
222 Waverly Place, Manhattan, NY 10014
(212) 691-1287

ITALY ❹

Bella Blu
967 Lexington Avenue, New York, NY 10021
(212) 988-4624

LEBANON ❽

Ilili Restaurant
236 5th Avenue, New York, NY 10001
(212) 683-2929

MEXICO ㉑

La Esquina
114 Kenmare Street, New York, NY 10012
(646) 613-1333

MOROCCO ⓱

Café Mogador
101 St Marks Place, New York, NY 10009
(212) 677-2226

PERU ❼

Pio Pio
604 10th Avenue, New York, NY 10036
(212) 459-2929

PHILIPPINES ㉕

Pig and Khao
68 Clinton Street, New York, NY 10002
(212) 920-4485

POLAND 16

Veselka
144 2nd Avenue, New York, NY 10003
(212) 228-9682

RUSSIA 24

Mari Vanna
41 E 20th St, New York, NY 10003
(212) 260-5775

SCANDINAVIA 14

Aquavit
65 E 55th St, New York, NY 10022
(212) 203-2121

SPAIN 9

Café Riazor
245 West 16th Street, New York, NY 10011
(212) 727-2132

THAILAND 1

Thai Market
960 Amsterdam Avenue, Manhattan, NY 10025
(212) 280-4575

TIBET 15

Mamak
174 2nd Avenue, New York, NY 10003

VIETNAM 22

Pho Grand
277 Grand Street, New York, NY 10002
(212) 965-5366

Central Park

Hudson River

MANHATTAN
MIDTOWN

DOWNTOWN

UPTOWN

BRONX

East River

2

QUEENS

BROOKLYN

AROUND THE WORLD

1. *Thailand*
2. *Germany*
3. *Czech Republic*
4. *Italy*
5. *Belgium*
6. *Ethiopia*
7. *Peru*
8. *Lebanon*
9. *Spain*
10. *Israel*
11. *Egypt*
12. *Jamaica*
13. *Cuba*
14. *Scandinavia*
15. *Tibet*
16. *Poland*
17. *Morocco*
18. *India*
19. *Argentina*
20. *Australia*
21. *Mexico*
22. *Vietnam*
23. *Austria*
24. *Russia*
25. *Philippines*

DIVE BARS

The gentrification of New York is an accepted fact, and while the grittiness of the city many of us grew up with may have become overrun with flashy fusion food restaurants and plush lounges serving specialty cocktails, the dive bar remains a connection to a past many of us cherish. There are certain generalizations that people like to make about dive bars, specifically that they are filthy places, covered in Christmas lights and stinking of stale beer, and that they only serve cheap drinks and horrible bar food. But what they ignore, and what draws people to these places, is that a dive bar has an unpretentious attitude about it. Bartenders will either get friendly with you immediately or pretty much ignore you until you've been ordering the same beer from them for years. If you're looking for a great place to enjoy a stiff drink or a cold beer, these no-frills bars are where to do it.

Doc Holliday's

141 Avenue A, New York, NY 10009
(212) 979-0132

From the fading mural of the Old West gunfighters outside to the Johnny Cash and Willie Nelson playing jukebox inside, Doc Holliday's is an East Village institution that defies the norms of the traditional Manhattan watering hole. The mood here is more festive than in your average dive, with bartenders dancing on the bar below the cowboy boots nailed to the ceiling and the admittedly frat-boyish crowd cheering along as they down $2 PBR cans and shots of whiskey. Nonetheless, outside of those times when you would expect a bar to be packed and crazy, Doc's remains an enjoyable place to grab a drink and shoot some pool.

169 Bar

169 East Broadway, New York, NY 10002
(646) 833-7199

The bouncers at the door of 169 Bar aren't there for decoration. They're serious about keeping out the rough element that characterized this Lower East Side institution that's been open in one form or another for almost a century. While the old lady bartenders who once kept the Bowery bums company are long gone, 169 remains a satisfyingly obscure place to get a beer-and-shot combo for $3 and play a couple games of pool. And though you can eat oysters until 4am, they also offer an extensive selection of food that's deep-fried to oblivion so that no one forgets exactly what kind of joint they're.

Trash

1471 First Avenue, New York, NY 10075
(212) 988-9008

For those who want the rock n' roll attitude, complete with motorcycle gas tanks and pictures of hotrods and scantily clad ladies on the walls, Trash is the place to be. The walls may be covered with kitsch, from go-karts to snowboards, but the space itself rarely is. In a quiet part of the Upper East Side, Trash is an honest dive bar, a place to grab cheap pints of Bud Light and shoot a few games of pool while the jukebox pumps out heavy metal and classic rock. Live music performances attract people from the area as well as biker-types from all over.

Lucy's

135 Avenue A, Manhattan, NY 10009
(212) 673-3824

You could recognize Lucy's solely from the films that have been shot here, but for the regulars, it's the owner, Lucy Valosky, that makes you keep coming back. She's the one, night after night, along with her daughter and granddaughter, hustling behind the bar pouring stiff drinks and feeding the jukebox. In addition to $3 beers, there are two pool tables (free!) and a pinball machine to entertain a much more laid back clientele than what you find in the rest of the newly hip neighborhood.

Vazac's Horseshoe Bar 7B°

Vazac's Horseshoe Bar (7B)

108 Avenue B, New York, NY 10009
(212) 677-6742

Filled with rickety booths and graffiti on the wall, Horseshoe Bar (also known as 7B after the corner it's on) is an extremely laid-back and friendly place. 7B, which has had roles in *Sex and the City, Serpico* and *The Godfather, Part II*, is frequented by people of all types and ages who enjoy a relaxed drinking session. The bar itself is impressive, long enough for over 30 taps of beer (the bottle selection is also extensive). There are also two pinball machines, a photo booth and a jukebox with a killer punk selection. A sign above the bar that reads, "Be nice or leave!" says it all about this place.

Alibi

242 Dekalb Avenue, Brooklyn, NY 11205
(718) 789-7100

This anonymous dive bar in Brooklyn attracts a diverse crowd of old regulars, locals from the Fort Green neighborhood, and, during the school year, plenty of art students from nearby Pratt Institute. With a pool table, Big Buck Hunter, bad movies looped in the background and an insane happy hour deal usually consisting of pretty much all drinks for 3 or 4 bucks, it's easy to understand how this bar has survived, and barely changed at all, since the Great Depression.

People from all over the country would probably take serious offense to someone championing New York as the capital of BBQ, but I done did it. While all of Texas, cities like Memphis or Kansas City, and countless smaller towns somewhere green may each have their specialties, in New York, we have it all. Not only do we take the best of the best from around the country, nay, the world, in New York, where the competition to survive, stand out, our pit masters have to constantly be on top of their game. New York is in the throes of a BBQ renaissance, and true carnivore will find his delight in any of these places.

Daisy May's BBQ

623 11th Avenue, New York, NY 10036
(212) 977-1500

Adam Perry Lang, a veteran of Daniel and Le Cirque, left the fine dining world to open a little BBQ shack in a dead zone way out west where his team smokes 2000 pounds of meat a day and simply closes shop when the last ribs are sold. An early lunch is the best way to go about getting your hands on his award winning Sweet & Sticky pork ribs or a simple yet satisfyingly scrumptious saucy Carolina pulled pork sandwich. There's nothing fancy about Daisy May's: you'll order your food at the counter and carry it over yourself to one of the big picnic tables in the back. Also perfect for big groups, the whole hogs (up to 30 pounds) you can order in advance (do it!).

Might Quinn's Barbeque

103 2nd Avenue, New York, NY 10003
(212) 677-3733

Hugh Mangum, a Jean-Georges disciple (that should mean something to some of you), opened this cafeteria-style restaurant in 2012 after making headlines with his stands at Smorgasburg, Brooklyn's food market. Mighty Quinn's produces what is probably the best pulled pork in the city, thanks to the all-Berkshire butts and the spicy yet balanced sauce that finishes them, but don't forget the massive beef rib with its serious bark and tender inside or the sandwich that dreams are made of, brisket piled high on a brioche bun with a squirt of sweet and sour sauce. Throw in a solid list of craft beers available by the cup or growler, plus thoughtful sides like *edamame* with goat cheese, and you've got yourself a contender for best BBQ in town.

Dinosaur Bar-B-Que

700 W 125th Street, New York, NY 10027
(212) 694-1777

Located in Harlem, Dinosaur is not as central as some other places, but for finger-licking good BBQ, and a raucous experience while you're at it, it's the way to go. Yes, it's a chain restaurant, but that doesn't detract from the quality of their BBQ. Dinosaur boasts two signature items: gigantic spice rubbed chicken wings and succulent savory pork ribs that fall off the bone. With incredible sides like fried green tomatoes and homemade baked beans to pair with them, it's probably best to make this a family affair and order one of everything.

Hill Country BBQ Market

30 W 26th Street, New York, NY 10010
(212) 255-4544

Perhaps the most celebrated BBQ region in the United States, and Hill Country BBQ Market is an ode to this part of the Lone Star State. In true Texas style, the meat is ordered at a counter by the pound, served on butcher paper and enjoyed at communal tables. Fatty brisket, meaty spare ribs and plump sausages straight from the source (the Kreuz Market in Lockhart, Texas) should be consumed to your stomach's content before you head to the downstairs bar where you're likely to find a live band playing. Hill Country also hosts an all-you-can-eat night on Mondays for carnivores ready to handle epic amounts of BBQ.

Blue Smoke

116 E. 27th St, New York, NY 10016
(212) 447-7733

For nearly a decade and a half now hungry diners have been chowing down on platters of some of the city's best BBQ in a setting worthy of the place's pedigree: woody barroom full of red-vinyl booths, a skylit dining room, and a hot jazz club. Since 2014, executive chef Jean-Paul Bourgeois has been offering a "From the Pit" menu featuring spare ribs, babyback ribs, pulled pork shoulder, seven pepper rubbed brisket, pastrami rubbed shortrib, barbecue chicken and the "Rhapsody in Cue" combo with spares, pork, chicken and sausage, all coming out of a hickory smoker.

Fette Sau

354 Metropolitan Avenue, New York, NY 11211
(718) 963-3404

Housed in a converted garage, it only prepares a few different smoked meats each day, and you're going to be ordering by the pound. The selections here are eclectic too: pork belly, a rare find in the city's barbecue community, is a menu mainstay here, and Fette Sau was also the first outfit to experiment with a slow and low pastrami. If you happen to come on a day when lamb ribs, goat, or cheeks of either pork or wagyu beef are being served, don't be shy. Beer can be ordered by the pint and up to the gallon. The line for a table can get outrageous, so bring some friends to keep you company while you wait get psyched to feast.

LINCOLN CENTER AND THE MET

Lincoln Center is one of New York's most iconic cultural institutions, home to 11 resident organizations that present New Yorkers with performances in symphony, opera, theater, dance, film and more. The main attraction is undoubtedly the Metropolitan Opera House, known around the world simply as The Met, but since 1959, Lincoln Center has been the driving creative force behind the cultural beat of the city, and from the New York Film Festival at the Walter Reade Theater to the New York City Ballet at the David H. Koch Theater, it continues to attract many of the world's premier artists to its stages.

The Met is perhaps the most spectacular place in the world to experience an opera or ballet, and it's no coincidence that it's where Luciano Pavarotti decided to bid farewell to opera forever. All the great divas have performed here, from Maria Callas and Joan Sutherland to Renata Tebaldi and Beverly Sills. The space hosts the Metropolitan Opera from September to May, but during the rest of the year showcases works from a range of international dance companies, including the Paris Opéra Ballet and the Kirov Ballet. When it comes to production value, some shows at the Met can make the very best of Broadway seem shabby, and even if you attend a performance devoid of international stars, an evening at this opera house is always an event.

Some of the other events held at Lincoln Center throughout the year include "Lincoln Center Out of Doors", a free festival in August that presents all kinds of performances including world music, dance, performance art and jazz, and the "Mostly Mozart Festival", an annual month long festival that celebrates the music of Mozart, Beethoven, Schubert, Haydn and other maestros.

In addition, because of Lincoln Center's prime location on the Upper West Side, there are numerous options for a pre or post performance dinner. To make the most of a fancy night out on the town, a table at Bar Boulud, Daniel Boulud's informal restaurant focusing on wine and charcuterie that has no equal in New York is always a great choice, especially since it is located directly

Lincoln Center

across the street and the charcuterie is courtesy of an acolyte of famous French charcuterie master Gilles Verot. Telepan, located inside a classic Upper West Side brownstone on 69th Street, serves amazing seafood dishes and has an eclectic wine list, especially in its "New World" section. And finally, a permanent draw for patrons of Lincoln Center, Shun Lee serves consistently delicious Chinese food in a cool retro setting, complete with distinctive wraparound wall dragon and glossy black booths.

Lincoln Center

10 Lincoln Center Plaza, New York, NY 10023
lc.lincolncenter.org

Bar Boulud

1900 Broadway, New York, NY 10023
(212) 595-0303

Telepan

72 West 69th Street, New York, NY 10023
(212) 580-4300

Shun Lee

43 West 65th Street, New York, NY 10023
(212) 769-3888

UPPER EAST SIDE SHOPPING

The Upper East Side of Manhattan is home to some of the world's most glamorous shops, jewelers and hair salons, as well as some of its most iconic grand department stores.

Ranking above the Champs Elysées in Paris, 5th Avenue between 52nd and 58th Streets is the world's most expensive commercial real estate. The corner of 57th Street and 5th Avenue, marked by Louis Vuitton's flagship store on one corner, and Tiffany, Bvlgari and Van Cleef & Arpels on the others, holds the title.

Madison Avenue, between 57th and 80th Streets, often referred to as the "Gold Coast" of shopping, has what it takes to satisfy the needs of a shopaholic, with the added bonus of benefitting from the fact that adjacent 5th Avenue attracts the hordes of tourists. Some non top-designer spots to check out on Madison Avenue:

Milly

900 Madison Avenue, New York, NY 10021
(212) 395-9100

Schutz

655 Madison Avenue, New York, NY 10065
(212) 257-4366

Alexis Bittar

1100 Madison Avenue, New York, NY 10028
(212) 249-3581

And then there are the Upper East Side's three department stores, the "three B's", where you can spend an entire afternoon brand hopping without having to walk a foot of sidewalk.

The corner of 5th and 57th

Barneys New York

660 Madison Avenue, New York, NY 10065
(212) 826-8900

High fashion fans able to afford it take advantage of the boutiques at Barneys New York. Presenting only the trendiest of what New York's department stores have to offer, Barneys' biannual sales even allow smaller budget shoppers the opportunity to get their fix. The ground floor offers an excellent selection of accessories – think Hermes watches and Pucci scarves - while the shoe department offers almost everything that exists from Manolo Blahnik and Miu Miu.

Bergdorf Goodman

754 5th Avenue, New York, NY 10019
(212) 753-7300

Located in the former Vanderbilt Mansion, you'll find luxury clothing, housewares and accessories at Bergdorf Goodman. The store offers great names synonymous with elegance like Carolina Herrera and Ralph Lauren, but also styles that are a little more "edgy" such as Proenza Schouler and Doo Ri. Renowned for its top shelf goods, the store has nevertheless expanded their inventory to include items for a younger, hipper clientele. The men's store is located across the street.

Bloomingdale's

1000 3rd Avenue, New York, NY 10022
(212) 705-2000

Considered one of the city's many tourist attractions, Bloomingdale's is certainly one of New York's most important institutions. Even the most seasoned professionals may feel overwhelmed by the vast choice on offer here. From handbags to beauty products, home décor to designer clothing, everything you could want is at most an elevator ride away. In addition, there are often crazy sales to take advantage of. For a little snacking in between purchases, gelato from 40 Carrots on the 7th floor or cupcakes from Magnolia Bakery on the ground floor can replenish your strength so you can make it through all 8 floors of shopping without fainting.

TRANSPORTATION

There are plenty of overpopulated cities in the world with astonishing traffic problems, but Manhattan, despite having over 1.6 million people living on less than 23 square miles (the five boroughs in 2015 counted over 8.5 million on just about 200 square miles), still manages to make getting around town relatively hassle free.

New York's legendary yellow taxis, all 14,000 of them, zig zag through the streets 24 hours a day, although you'll be lucky to find one willing to pick you up during the unfortunately timed 4-5pm shift change window.

The city is also proud to have one of the world's oldest and most expansive subway systems. Nearly 6 million rides are taken every weekday and about half of that number on weekends. It's easily the most efficient way to travel from one end of the city to the other, and the number of riders keeps increasing as the cost of gas and taxi fares go up.

The city's grid layout is also easy to navigate by bus, with nearly every avenue taking riders north and south and most

major cross streets providing east and west options. But cabs can get stuck in traffic, buses can be slow, and the subways can be cramped like sardine cans.

Finally, as of 2013, New Yorkers have another mode of transportation available to them. The bike share program has finally hit the Big Apple. Blue Citi Bikes are now as part of the traffic landscape as anything, an instantly recognizable symbol of New York.

The program launched in 2013 with over 6,000 bikes at 330 stations in Brooklyn and Manhattan, and by 2017, Citi Bike plans to double its fleet to 12,000 bikes and continue expanding its docking stations to accommodate the roughly 100,000 users taking nearly 40,000 trips

per day. For tourists, the bright blue Citi Bikes are a convenient way to explore the city and for locals, they've become the cheapest and fastest way to get from A to B, and that's without getting into the green aspect of it all, so let's hope the biking trend in the city continues.

ONE SPOT PER HOOD

Generally speaking, it's pretty difficult to get lost in the city, but it's definitely a good thing to step out of your comfort zone every now and again to explore those neighborhoods you don't get a chance to frequent too often. When that time comes, it's always good to have at least one go-to spot in your back pocket. Whether it's a bar or a store, a park or a museum, when I find myself in the following neighborhoods, whether it be by chance or if I just have a little time to kill, I'll usually end up at one of these places.

HARLEM

Rucker Park

W 155th street & 8th Ave, Manhattan, NY 10039

Some of the NBA's best honed their skills on this park's court and some occasionally come back during the off-season.

SPANISH HARLEM

Patsy's

2287 1st Ave, New York, NY 10035

One of the city's first pizzerias, in a neighborhood that once represented Italy in New York.

UPPER EAST SIDE

Mel's Burger

1450 2nd Ave, New York, NY 10021

A fun neighborhood bar that attracts the locals for its selection of 20 burgers, including the "Fat Mexican" and the "Dirty Hipster" as well it's 24 beers on tap, a perfect accompaniment to the games on the flat screens.

MIDTOWN

Moma Garden

11 W 53rd Street, New York, NY 10019

Access to the sculpture garden at the Museum of Modern Art is reserved for those who've purchased admission to the museum, but to take a breather and escape the Midtown crowds, there is no better remedy in the area.

MURRAY HILL

Waterfront Ale House

540 2nd Avenue, New York, NY 10016

It's impossible not to stop by this bar, either before or after catching a flick at the Kips Bay movie theater across the street, for a bowl of their banging chili, a few drinks, or just to take one of their bottles of homemade hot sauce to go.

GRAMERCY

Rose Bar @ Gramercy Hotel

2 Lexington Avenue, New York, NY 10010

One of the most luxurious hotel bars in the city, it can sometimes be difficult to get in to this gorgeous space filled with artwork and a one-of-a-kind Maarten Bass billiards table, but it's always worth a shot.

EAST VILLAGE

Crif Dogs

113 St Marks Pl, New York, NY 10009

A hole-in-the-wall spot that serves hot dogs in ways you've never imagined, the décor consists of action figurines and arcade games, while PDT, one of the city's top notch cocktail bars, can be accessed through a telephone booth inside.

LITTLE ITALY

Parm

248 Mulberry St, New York, NY 10012

A casual restaurant and sandwich shop famous for its eponymous sandwiches, either eggplant, chicken, or meatball. Sit or take to go, either way your stomach is happy.

LOWER EAST SIDE

Katz's Deli

205 East Houston Street, New York, NY 10002

Pastrami on rye is an iconic New York sandwich, and ever since Meg Ryan's epic scene in *When Hary Met Sally*, people from around the world have been lining up for a heaping portion of what I consider to be the city's very best.

FINANCIAL DISTRICT

Stone Street

No single spot here, so it's best to start at one end of the street and eat and drink your way to the other. When it's nice out and the tables are set up on the cobblestoned street, the ambiance is second to none.

TRIBECA

Brandy Library

25 N. Moore St, New York, NY 10013

No books, but a ton of booze lining the walls. Normal, since the drinks menu lists almost every liquor you can think of, plus over 100 different cocktails. Shell out $13 bucks on one of those and you'll get your drink and a basket of gougères (warm cheese puffs).

WEST VILLAGE

Fat Cat

75 Christopher Street, New York, NY 10014

A below-ground bar mostly frequented by NYU students, Fat Cat has dozens of ping pong and pool tables, as well as various other games, and the bar sells PBR by the 12-pack so you don't have to keep interrupting your game.

CHELSEA

Sleep No More

530 W 27th Street, New York, NY 10001

A play, based on Macbeth, where the audience wears masks, aren't allowed to speak, and are guided in groups through the twenty-plus rooms in which the play

unfolds. Definitely a unique experience not to be missed, so make that reservation now.

THEATER DISTRICT

Russian Vodka Room

265 W 52nd Street, New York, NY 10019

New Yorker's avoid Times Square like the plague, but if I'm in the area to catch a play on Broadway, I'll definitely hop in for a few shots of their infused vodkas wither before or after the show.

UPPER WEST SIDE

Shalel Lounge

65 West 70th Street, New York, NY 10023

There's a little staircase illuminated by votive candles you'll have to find to get

to this Moroccan-inspired bar. Once downstairs, there are several "caves" carved into the stone and filled with cushions where you'll appreciate good tunes, shared plates, wines and cocktails.

MORNINGSIDE HEIGHTS

Fairway

2328 12th Avenue, New York, NY 10027

Most of the city is short on space to host a huge market, but in this neighborhood, Fairway managed to create one of the largest supermarkets in town.
The place has everything you could ask for, including giant winter coats for you to wear when you enter the temperature controlled meat and fish departments.

CENTRAL PARK

The Loeb Central Park Boat House

East 72nd Street and 5th Avenue, New York, NY 10021

When you want something more than a picnic in the park, a romantic boat ride on the lake will inevitably bring on an appetite you can satisfy at the Boathouse.

The Loeb Central Park Boat House

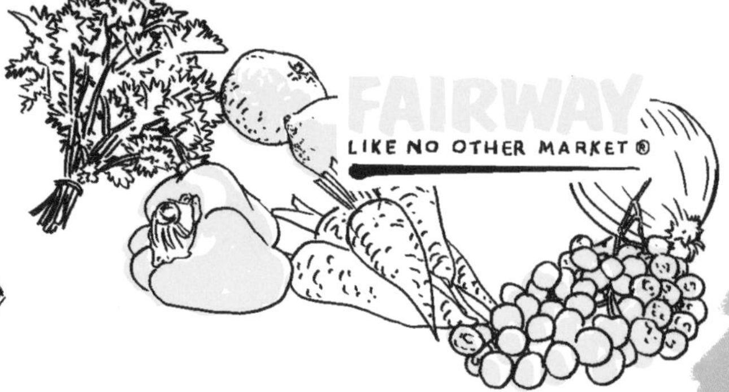
FAIRWAY
LIKE NO OTHER MARKET ®

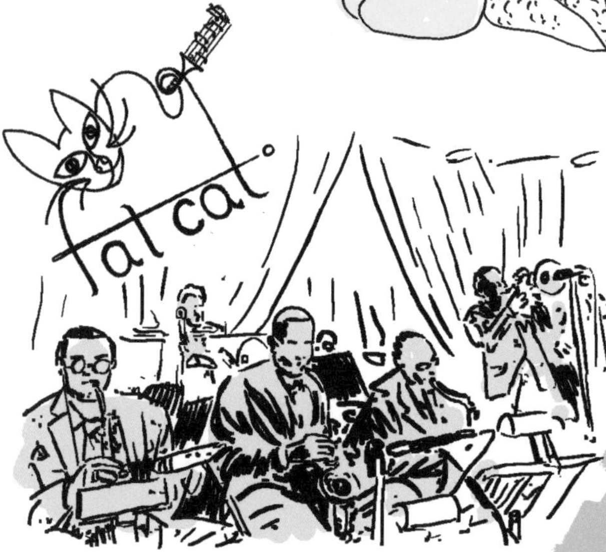
fat cat

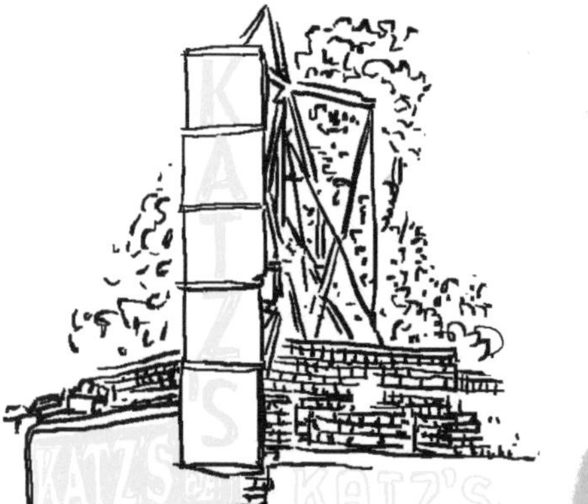
KATZ'S
KATZ'S
KATZ'S

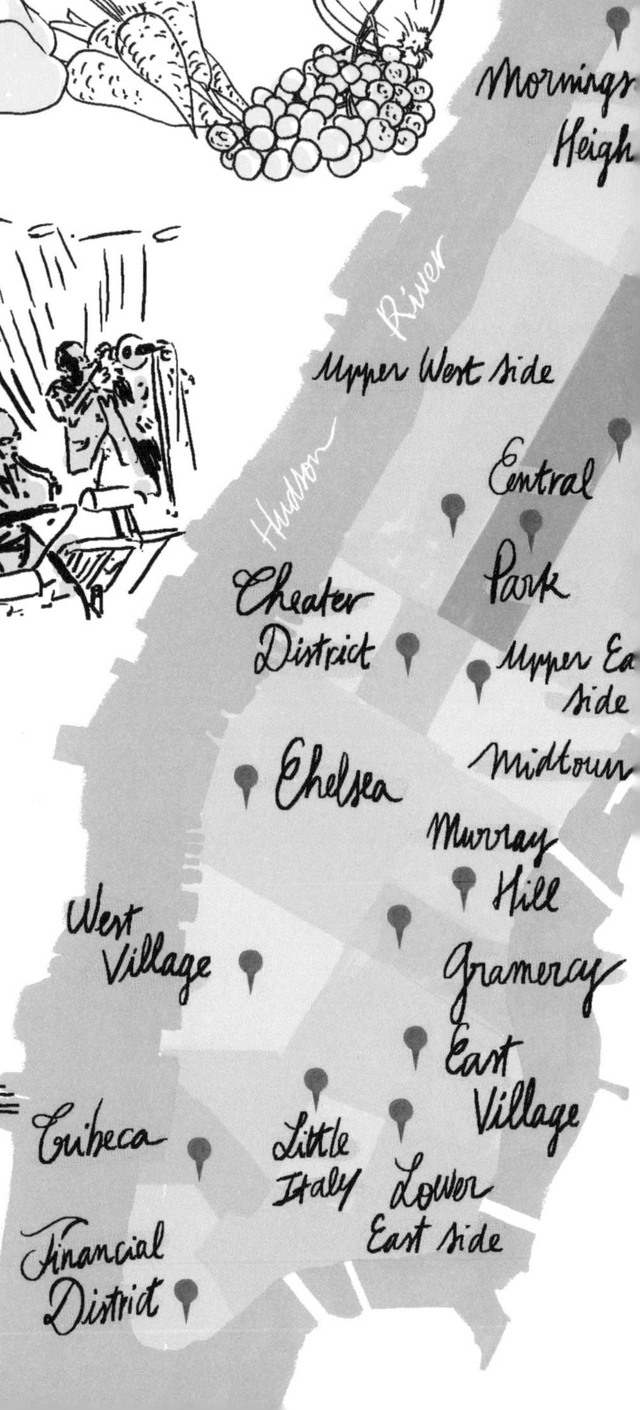
Mornings
Heigh
Hudson River
Upper West side
Central Park
Theater District
Upper Ea side
Midtown
Chelsea
Murray Hill
West Village
Gramercy
East Village
Tribeca
Little Italy
Lower East side
Financial District

HOLCOMBE RUCKER PLAYGROUND

Harlem

East River

East Harlem

Patsy's SINCE 1933

Yorkville

NYC'S #1 WEINER

CRIF★DOGS

RUSSIAN VODKA ROOM SINCE 1997

TODARO'S ITALIAN SPECIALTIES, N.Y.

The Freedom Tower standing tall

The Roosevelt Island tram

The Brooklyn Bridge at night

NYC taxis

Downtown Manhattan

The Plaza

OPEN 24HRS

New York has a reputation for being the city that never sleeps. If some areas have matured and now enjoy a more peaceful rest, night owls shouldn't worry as there are still plenty of out of the norm fun things to do at all hours of the night. Of course, nightclubs worldwide now have parties that last until dawn, but only in New York can you leave said party and still have a plethora of things to do. Every corner has a bodega or diner open 24 hours, but here are a few more interesting options that attract New Yorkers at the end of a lively night out on the town.

Space Billiards

34 West 32nd Street, New York, NY, 10001
(212) 239-4166

Located on the 12th floor of a random office building in Koreatown, the name given to the part of 32nd Street overflowing with Korean restaurants and shops, Space Billiards is a clean, spacious and well lit (by the neon beer signs) pool hall. This spot is really for serious players willing to brave an uncertain elevator to play up on that 12th floor, but it also attracts those for whom a 6am game of pool, regular or Korean, just seems a natural prolongation to a night out on the town. An emergency exit opens onto a staircase outside where smokers can enjoy a beautiful view of the Empire State Building rising just above.

Wo Hop

17 Mott Street, New York, NY, 10013
(212) 962-8617

Wo Hop is a Chinese restaurant at the very end of Chinatown's Mott Street, a dimly lit winding street where you can easily imagine a gangster film, or just a gangster, being shot. A shady staircase leads to an underground dining area usually filled with Chinese people on one side, neighborhood cops on the other, and between all that, the intoxicated masses in need of a noodle dish or some roast pork to help restore balance. The food is authentic and delicious, and not just for five in the morning when you're body is willing to devour everything and anything.

Gray's Papaya

2090 Broadway, New York, NY 10023
(212) 799-0243

Hot dogs can be found on almost every street corner in Manhattan. These "dirty water dogs" as they're not so affectionately referred to, don't compare, neither in quality nor affordability, to what Gray's Papaya on the Upper West Side has been serving since the 70's. The "papaya" in the name refers to the papaya drink sold here, often in combination with two hot dogs, which is still called the "Recession Special" and costs less than 5 bucks. The hot dogs are grilled and served in a warm bun, delivering a perfect crunch with each bite, even under a pile of sauerkraut or onions, both available free of charge. Whether it's noon or midnight, no visit to the Upper West Side is complete without stopping by the Gray's counter for a quick order.

Staten Island Ferry

Whitehall Ferry Terminal
4 South Street, Battery Park, Manhattan

The Staten Island ferry departs every half hour, every 20 minutes at peak hours. After a long night of partying it up in a downtown club, you grab a breakfast sandwich to go from any bodega or corner cart and jump on this free boat ride with amazing views of the tip of the island, the Statue of Liberty and the sunrise, seemingly all for you. Honestly, it's a magical and unforgettable moment.

Chorus Karaoke

25 West 32nd Street, 3rd Floor, New York, NY 10001
(212) 967-2244

A few steps from Space Billiards, you'll find Chorus Karaoke, a place that invites you to sing your heart out until dawn. A main room with a stage and bar welcomes solo and group singers who just want a drink and to sing some songs, while private rooms can be rented by the hour for larger groups or special events. A good selection of songs (American and Korean) and beers makes it a favorite destination for lovers of karaoke.

Grand Morelos

727 Grand Street, Brooklyn, NY 11211
(718) 218-9441

Grand Morelos in Williamsburg offers the perfect menu for late night munchies after the local bars have closed. Sure, you can find typical American diner fare like juicy burgers and thick milkshakes, but the true deliciousness lies in the Mexican selections, including a wide variety of *tortas, fajitas* with beef or chicken, and a delicious *guacamole*. A friendly piece of advice: the spicy green sauce goes with everything. The food is all prepared fresh, with even the chips arriving at the table still warm. In addition, the place doubles as a bakery, so you can take more of their famous "tres leches" cake to go when you're done chowing down at the table.

Index of addresses by theme

LES GUIDES DU CHÊNE

DES GUIDES PAS COMME LES AUTRES

ALREADY AVAILABLE IN ENGLISH :

Paris for men
Thierry Richard, Aseyn,
Juliette Ranck

The first city guide for men
who love Paris.

My Little Paris
My Little Paris, Kanako

The Paris only Parisians know!

My Sweet Paris

Caroline Mignot, Pierre-Olivier Signe

The Top 150 places for Dessert
in Paris

Paris by Bike with Velib

Bicycle Hides around Paris

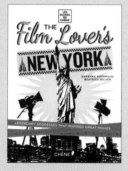

The film lover's New York

Barbara Boespflug, Beatrice Billon, Pierre-Olivier Signe

60 legendary addresses that
inspired great movies.

The film lover's Paris

Barbara Boespflug, Beatrice Billon, Pierre-Olivier Signe

101 legendary adresses that
inspired great movies.

Thank You

New York is nothing without New Yorkers, and this book wouldn't be possible without them.

Of the 8 million plus people that call NYC home, I have to single out and give special thanks to Rocky and Dusty. Thanks guys not just for the gorgeous photos in this book but for the years of friendship we've shared and those to come.

Robbie and Laura London, my confidants slash therapists, you kept me sane during the writing of both versions of this book, and for that and everything else I am eternally grateful.

When I think of New York, my New York, and especially my New Yorkers, I'm thinking about the team of friends that made discovering and taking advantage of this city the amazing adventure it was.

You guys were with me every step of the way, from the basement bars to the rooftop lounges and everything in between, and without the likes of you, this city wouldn't have the energy it does and I wouldn't be the person I am. You know who you are.

Last, but certainly not least, this book is for my baby girl, Louise, in the hope that one day you get to know and love the city that made me, and in turn crush it like I know you will.

© 2016, Editions du Chêne - Hachette Livre or the English edition
© 2014, Editions du Chêne - Hachette Livre for the original edition
www.editionsduchene.fr

Editor: Volcy Loustau
Artistic Director: Sabine Houplain with the collaboration of Claire Mieyeville
Layout and Graphic Design: Gaëlle Junius
Drawings on cover and pages 15, 110-111, 132-133: © Aseyn
Photos: © Alex Ramniceanu, © David Brodeur
Proofreader: Myriam Blanc
Photogravure: Quat'Coul
English layout: Emilie Serralta
Sales and partnerships: Mathilde Barrois
mbarrois@hachette-livre.fr
Press Relations: Hélène Maurice
hmaurice@hachette-livre.fr

Published by Éditions du Chêne
(58 rue Jean Bleuzen, CS 70007, 92178 Vanves Cedex)
Printed in Spain by Estella Graficas
Copyright Registration: September 2016
ISBN 978-2-81231-533-6
24/8487/2